What Writers are saying

Soul Care for Writers

As a writer, you can often feel isolated and alone with the daunting task of unleashing the creative within. Soul Care for Writers helps to explore the hidden fears and temptations that can plague a writer. From the moment I scanned the table of contents, I found that the author seems to have a sixth sense of what I wrestle with in my writing nearly every day. With gentle prodding and creative exercises, Edie helps move you from feeling stifled to understanding how to release the flow of words through centering yourself in God, the giver of the gift. Each chapter is skillfully designed to help you flourish and wield your influence from a God-centered approach with prayer, reflection, and creativity. *Soul Care for Writers* needs to be on every writers bookshelf whether beginner or seasoned author.

~Cynthia Cavanaugh, Award Winning Author,
Speaker, Life Coach

Once a writer discovers the connection between faith and creativity, the creative juices begin to flow. In *Soul Care for Writers,* Edie Melson has done a superb job of taking writers on a journey to discover this connection. Through her own personal experiences, lists, and suggested exercises, Melson leaves nothing to your imagination. Just follow her instruction and you will find enrichment for your writing life, a deeper sense of your calling to write, a closeness with the Author of the Word, and creative inspiration as ideas fill your mind.

~Linda Gilden, Conference director, editor, and
writing coach. Author of the *LINKED® Quick Guides to
Personalities, Articles, Articles, Articles!* and more

Edie's soul-searching book crashes through the walls of the writer's insecurities and stamps out fear through sound biblically-based exercises. Any writer questioning whether God is still calling them to write needs *Soul Care for Writers.*

~Emme Gannon, Writer

I wish *Soul Care for Writers* had been around when I began my writing career. It would have saved me a lot of gray hairs! That's why I'm so glad that Edie Melson is sharing her wealth of wisdom with all of us. It will be an invaluable resource on those days when we wonder why we didn't choose an easier career like chainsaw-juggling—and a deep encouragement as we remain faithful to the calling God's placed on our lives.

~Michelle Cox, author of the *When God Calls the Heart to Love series* and *Just 18 Summers*

As an author, speaker, and photographer, Edie Melson understands creatives – both our desire to encourage others with the words we write, as well as the particular stresses we face. In *Soul Care for Writers*, Melson confronts struggles writers face, like doubt, fear, comparison, and then invites us to nourish our hearts and minds through creativeness and prayer. This is a practical, hope-filled book that I highly recommend – one I can't wait to use to refresh my own soul.

~Beth K. Vogt, Christy-Award-winning author

Edie Melson delivers encouragement to writers everywhere in *Soul Care for Writers*. Don't quit your writing dream before reading and doing the exercises in this gem of a book. She delivers refreshment alongside practical exercises for your soul.

~Alycia W. Morales, author

Soul Care for Writers is not just geared towards the "seasoned" writer, but it is also for those beginning their writing journey. Edie so brilliantly emanates her words by bringing light to the darkest places of our writing ... fear and doubt. Thoughtful prompts though-out the book will leave you eager to see what the next chapter holds. These creative connections, in Edie's words, "Allow God's creative genius to inspire us and replace fear with creativity." This book is a must read to anyone ready to embark on the journey as a serious writer.

~Andrea J. Tomassi, Founder, Transcended Ministries Co-Author, *Live Bold Devotional Journal*

Soul Care for Writers is an essential resource for unpublished and published writers alike. Edie Melson has mentored many writers, myself included, and she knows the unique struggles that writers face. With warmth, transparency, and wisdom, Edie shines a gentle light on the fears and doubts that stifle our creativity. *Soul Care for Writers* is a beacon of hope, guiding weary writers to the One who created us, who called us to write, and who understands our soul-level creative weariness better than anyone.

~Lynn Blackburn, award-winning author

I'm a writer. Some days that's all I do for hours on end. As a result, I often feel worn out, tired, drained, empty. *Soul Care for Writers* is like a sip of water to a parched throat and a shot of energy to a flagging spirit. It's a great way to spend time renewing, refreshing, and replenishing after I've drained my emotional and creative well by pouring out everything into my fiction story. I highly recommend this book.

~Lynette Eason, best-selling, award-winning author of the Blue Justice Series.

Soul Care for Writers

Love & Blessings

Edie Melson

Ps 37:23-24

Soul Care For Writers

Edie Melson

Bold Vision Books
PO Box 2011
Friendswood, Texas 77549

Table of Contents

Dedication

This book is gratefully dedicated to
all the writers who have gone before,
making the path smooth for
the rest of us.
You've mentored each of us in
ways you'll never know and
I pray God reveals how you've
encouraged so many!

Acknowledgments

No author creates a book alone. We band together with editors, designers, and other writers who help and encourage us throughout the process. For this book though, there are some special people I'd like to thank.

First and foremost is my amazing partner in life, my husband Kirk Melson. He's my constant encourager, prayer warrior and best friend. Without him, I wouldn't be a writer.

I also want to thank those in my life who have given much needed—daily—prayer support. DiAnn Mills, Lynette Eason, Beth Vogt, Cynthia Cavanaugh, Rhonda Rhea, Molly Jo Realy, Tammy Karasek, Alycia Morales, Lynn Blackburn, Linda Gilden, Emme Gannon, and Erynn Newman. Also my More Than Sunday ladies accountability group, my AWSA Mastermind Group, and The Light Brigade.

A special thank you always goes to my amazing agent, David Van Diest. His wisdom and support make it possible for me to write with confidence.

Of course I want to give a shout out to everyone at Bold Vision Books. In particular I'm honored to work with Karen Porter. She caught the vision I had for this project and continues to help me shape it into what God has planned.

I could never leave out my sons and daughters, Jimmy and Katie Melson, Kirk and Weslyn Melson, and John Melson and Ayla Johnson. You have always believed in me and been among my staunchest supporters. Finally, one of my most loyal supporters is my precious sister, Katy Schneider. Her confidence in me knows no bounds, and she shouts it to the world. Everyone should have a sister like her!

Foreword

Writing is a product of the soul, a divine commission purposed by the God of the universe. The process involves the writer and the Creator working together to communicate truth, guidance, values, wisdom, and entertainment through uniquely formed words. The process is an opportunity for our dreams to go wild while exploring the Author of the universe.

Writers are dreamers. Need proof? Check out the Psalms. David's heartfelt words proclaim his love for God while he often wrestled with a myriad of emotions. Those same conflicting emotions, resulting from living in a pagan world, still plague us today. David's words inspire and encourage us to be better people and grow closer to God. We are warmed by a kinship of written communication.

Writers feel more intently. We experience the world in ways that demonstrate mankind's innate need for significance, security, and relationships. We long to weave the three together and point every reader to the cross. Each book we publish is launched on a mission trip to influence the reader.

The call to write is more than a passion; it's a ministry that unites us to each other and the great

Creator. The need within us to create shouts, even stalks us. Often it seems the consequences for our refusal to write, means death for the soul. We require Soul Care to survive the piercing arrows of rejection, the loneliness of developing our art in solitude, and the melancholia that can plague the creative personality.

Edie Melson's book delivers a blanket of peace, comfort, and serendipity to the writer. Let her techniques inspire you to step forward with confidence and assurance in your God-given purpose.

~DiAnn Mills, Best-selling author

Introduction

Those who write have opened themselves to specific stresses. We pull from what's inside us to create a gift. Our ultimate goals and dreams are as varied at the words we use. No matter why we write, I believe we each fight this battle to bring forth words to make the world a better place. We are hope givers, joy bringers, and light shiners.

To do this though, we must have something to pull from. Writing is an exhausting endeavor, and we cannot do it effectively when the well is dry. So this book points us to the One who understands us—and our craft—best.

God is the ultimate author, and it is His inheritance that we showcase when we put pen to paper. God planted a seed in each of us that bears the fruit of words. But this seed must be nurtured—shaded in the healing covering of His presence and watered by His spirit and His Word.

Our creative energy can be depleted, both outward and inward. In this volume, we'll rediscover ways to renew our reserves and reconnect with the One who called us to this endeavor.

Optional Supply List

My desire is for this book to be something you use. My prayer is that it will be become dog-eared and stained from carrying it around. I urge you to draw in it, experiment, and learn once again the healing power of play—especially play with our Heavenly Father.

You can use this book with nothing more than a pen or pencil. But if you want to go further, here is a list of supplies you might enjoy using:

- ☑ Colored Pencils
- ☑ Markers, fine tip, brush, and/or glitter
- ☑ Paint, acrylic and/or watercolor
- ☑ Washi Tape
- ☑ Stickers
- ☑ Gelato sticks
- ☑ Journal
- ☑ Glue
- ☑ Glitter
- ☑ Ribbon

In addition, there are several instances where I encourage you to take a photograph. You don't need special equipment.

- ☑ Cell phone camera
- ☑ An Instamatic of some kind, like Fujifilm Instax or Polaroid Snap
- ☑ Digital camera

Chapter One

Fighting Fear

Although it may not always be immediately obvious, a large portion of our struggles stem from fear. We're afraid of failure, trying something new, ridicule, the inability to perform, and sometimes even success. The list can go on and on. Until we unmask those fears and face them head-on, we're subject to an ambush that can totally derail our process.

I've struggled with these fears, and more. I've been beaten by fear, and I've triumphed over it. But the only place I've ever found to consistently ensure victory is closer to God. It's when I move closer to God and let His strength flow through me that I find I can always conquer fear.

During these times of closeness, His Spirit floods mine with truth. It's the truth of who I am— and more importantly Whose I am—that brings me relief. So this chapter will address our fears and bring them into the Light. We'll talk about the truth God has for us, pray for His protection, and most of all spend time creating with God in the safety of His protection.

Writing in the Light

For you were once darkness, but now you are light in
the Lord. Walk as children of light
Ephesians 5:8 (HCSB).

In addition to being a writer, I'm also a photographer. And one of the earliest lessons I learned about good photography was that exposure matters. I'll be non-technical: for an image to work, there has to be light—and plenty of it—or the picture won't look right. Not enough light means it's a blurry dark mess that's unrecognizable. No matter how much post editing we do to an underexposed picture, it can't be fixed.

Contrary to that, too much light will blow out a picture—littering an otherwise beautiful image with spots of bright white that can't be toned down.

I've discovered that developing a life of writing is a lot like finding the perfect exposure for a picture.

I can't do it in the dark. The dark is a scary place, and when I'm there, my fears take root and grow.

As a writer, trying to write in the dark means trying to compose my thoughts away from God. He's the light-bearer for my life. His insight and illumination brightens all that I write. When I don't spend time with Him—in prayer, Bible reading, and reflection—my words lose their shine.

The over-exposure that sometimes happens isn't too much God in my life. There can never be enough of God—ever. But that destructive light comes when I'm spending too much time in the false light of the world. I'm exposing myself to the lies that tell me I'll never be good enough, or keep up with the trends, or reach the people I want to reach. By bathing myself in the light of those lies, I destroy the composition I'm working toward with my words.

Now I'm working to compose my writing life with an eye toward the amount, and type, of light around me. Join me and let God use our words to bring light to a world that is dark.

Forging a Creative Connection

Yes, this is a book for writers, but this exercise doesn't start with the written word. Instead, we're going to observe and allow God's creative genius to inspire us and replace fear with creativity.

Here are the supplies you'll need:

- ☑ This book
- ☑ Access to the outdoors
- ☑ A notepad or journal
- ☑ Pen or pencil
- ☑ Optional
- ☑ Cell phone or regular camera

Begin by going outdoors. Find someplace where you can observe God's creation. That can be your backyard or a suburban garden. If you happen to be stuck in the city, just look up. The sky contains many of God's most beautiful masterpieces. Choose a place that's relatively quiet and has a place for you to sit.

Now look around. Really take time to study God's handiwork. Notice the colors, the smells, and the intricacy of all He's created. If you have a camera, take a few pictures. These photos aren't for Instagram™ but for your inspiration. Don't stress over how the photos look; instead use them as notes to jog your memory for the next step.

Write out your observations in your notepad or journal. This is a free-writing process. Don't hem yourself in with expectations or rules. Just write what you see. Then write how you feel—about yourself, this place and time, and God. Now take it one step further. Can any of these insights help you with a current project? Do they spawn a new idea? Write it down. Don't lose the gift God has just given you.

A Prayer
When Fear Closes In

Have I not commanded you? Be strong and courageous.
Do not be frightened, and do not be dismayed, for the
LORD your God is with you wherever you go
(Joshua 1:9 NASB).

Dear Lord, I find myself once again in a dark place with fear closing in on all sides. The only sights I see are the lies that swoop down on me when I try to find light. Everywhere I see examples of how inadequate I am. My writing isn't good enough, my platform is tiny, and every idea I have seems overdone. Now I've even begun to doubt the call you placed on my life.

Help me find the way out of this place. Shine a light in this darkness. Show me the truth of my situation. Remind me that the power of my words doesn't come from me, but from You working through me.

Don't let me continue to run from my fears. Show me how to face them and see them in the light of Your calling. I want to continue to learn and grow in the craft of writing. But I can't find a balance. It either feels like everything I write is worthless junk or precious jewels. Neither is accurate one hundred percent of the time.

Give me Your perspective as I move forward. Put others in my life who will help me evaluate what I'm writing objectively and without ulterior motives. Show me how to find a community I can trust.

Most of all, don't let me run from You and the call You whispered into my soul. Lead me through the doors that You open and give me peace to replace the fear. Amen.

We Can't Let Fear Stop Us

For God has not given us a spirit of fearfulness, but one of power, love, and sound judgment
(2 Timothy 1:7 HCSB).

I'd been stopped in my tracks for what seemed like days. My book deadline was looming, and still I couldn't make progress. The problem was I didn't know which way to turn. I was confused about the direction the book needed to go, and I'd allowed that confusion to open the door to fear and bring my writing to a screeching halt. The fear that I'd somehow already missed God or was on a path away from the direction God wanted for this particular book overwhelmed me.

I pushed myself back from my computer and changed into my walking shoes. I needed something to clear out the chaos and knew a walk with God would be just what the writing-doctor ordered. As I walked, I began talking to God. I laid out my thoughts, my struggle, and all the fears that had me tied in knots. As I talked, the fear faded and peace returned. Working issues out with God—out loud—had given me a hint about the direction to start moving again.

As I settled back at my desk, I started writing in that new direction. Sure enough, it didn't work. But, the fact that I was moving led me to discover the right road. That was the day I learned that not stopping was key to finding the right path. There will always be times when I'm confused or uncertain, now I will not let the fear of going the wrong direction stop me. God would—and has shown up—when needed.

Forging a Creative Connection

When fear presses in, sometimes it takes a change of scenery to give us the perspective we need. Here are the supplies you'll need:

- ☑ This book
- ☑ Access to a change of scenery (it can be different room or visiting a coffee shop)
- ☑ Pen or pencil
- ☑ Optional
- ☑ Colored Pencils, Markers and/or crayons
- ☑ Stickers
- ☑ Washi Tape

The idea behind this exercise is to change our perspective. I recommend visiting a coffee shop or somewhere you can get a refreshing drink. I prefer coffee, but sometimes I'm in the mood for tea. If you can't leave the house, make yourself something special to drink and move to a different location. Sit in a different chair, go to a different room, or take a seat on the grass outside.

It's easy to get bound up by our fears and shut down the joy of writing. Use the next page to write why you like being a writer and/or reasons you like to write. Nothing is off limits. See how many you can come up with. Then take some time and talk to God, thanking Him for the gift of writing in your life. Decorate the page.

A Prayer When I Can't Write

Do not be afraid, little flock, for your Father has chosen gladly to give you the kingdom (Luke 12:32 NASB).

Dear Lord, I'm so fearful of making a mistake or spending so much time going the wrong direction that I'll never catch back up. Help me overcome that fear with faith. You are my writing partner. Show me how to rely more fully on You when doubt stops me in my tracks.

Bring to mind all the times when You've helped me get redirected onto the better path. Don't let me look to my own ability to navigate. It's so easy for confusion and fear to send me into a doubt tornado.

Give me the faith I need to keep moving forward. Surround me with other writers who will encourage me. Let us band together for Your purpose, spurring one another on to a better craft and a closer walk with You.

Be my compass and my guide in all that I do with writing. Stop me from wasting time, but also don't let me be afraid to explore the unexpected twists and turns that you have for me. Renew my faith as you teach me how to keep moving. Amen.

When Failure Brings Blessings

That is why, for Christ's sake, I delight in weaknesses, in insults, in hardships, in persecutions, in difficulties. For when I am weak, then I am strong
(2 Corinthians 12:10 NIV).

For me, failure reinforces and validates the fears I battle as a writer. Every mistake I make seems to add weight to the voices I hear in my head that feed my insecurity. And I make a lot of mistakes. Because this vicious cycle can bring my writing to a screeching halt, I've had to find a way to combat this way of looking at life.

One week I was overwhelmed with assignments—blog posts, articles, devotions, and even a book—all due in the same week. Although I'd love to say I was organized and everything went off without a hitch, it didn't. The book I turned in had all my attention and the other assignments suffered. By the time Friday rolled around I felt like I'd been to war and back—finishing up wounded and weary. I'd been honest on social media about the craziness of the week and how I'd tried to make sure my work was typo-free and on time, but I'd fallen so short it was pathetic, and I knew it.

Truthfully, I felt like quitting that week. Everywhere I turned, the evidence of my failure was on view to the world. I couldn't see how my less-than-stellar work was blessing anyone. The last straw was the blog post I'd published on my own site that morning. As I read it in the email that had been sent out I just shook my head. The typos and other mistakes seemed to prove my ineptitude.

That was the day the email arrived in my inbox.

A new writer shared that although it had taken all her courage to write me, my openness about my struggles and my doubts that week had given her the push she needed. She felt I'd understand her turmoil. She went on to say that the fact I'd fallen short of perfection was an encouragement and was keeping her from quitting on the call God had placed on her life.

She shared her struggles, and I finished the email with tears in my eyes. How like God to show me once again how He was at work through me, no matter how imperfect I was. He reminded me that I wasn't the one who needed to be perfect. He has that covered—and in His perfection—He makes everything work together exactly as it should.

Forging a Creative Connection

Today we're going to create a Bible verse vision board. This project will help us focus on one idea, while highlighting what God has to say to us.

Here are the supplies you'll need:

- ☑ This book
- ☑ Pen or pencil
- ☑ Notepad or sketch pad
- ☑ Bible
- ☑ Colored Pencils, Markers, or Crayons
- ☑ Optional
- ☑ Stickers
- ☑ Washi tape

Choose **one** of the following Bible verses and write it across the top of your page of your notebook or sketchpad. Try to get the entire verse on one single line.

Philippians 4:13
Psalm 56:3
1 Chronicles 16:11

On that first line, highlight or color in the first word. As you do, ask God for insight into the meaning of the verse when the emphasis is on the first word.

Write the entire verse again on the second line. This time highlight or color the second word. As you do, ask God for insight into the meaning of the verse when the emphasis is on the second word.

Write the entire verse again on the third line. This time highlight or color the third word. As you do, ask God for insight into the meaning of the verse when the emphasis is on the third word.

Continue until you've highlighted every word in the verse.

Now decorate your page, and write any insights you've received so you don't forget them.

A Prayer When I Let Failure Make Me Doubt

And you must show mercy to those whose faith is wavering (Jude 1:22 NLT).

Dear Lord, I had such energy and hope when I first heard You whisper that I would be a writer. My imagination and dreams soared to all that calling would be. But now I'm no longer flying, instead I'm crawling through the mud of defeat and despair. Did I hear You wrong? Am I supposed to write for You or was it something I just made up?

Following You is all I've ever truly wanted. Help me grow into the person You designed me to be. Don't let my expectations get in the way of hearing Your voice. Replace the false ones with the calling that allows me to be exactly who You made me to be.

Speak to me. Let me clearly hear what Your plan is for my life. I don't feel like I'm getting anywhere with writing. I wonder how You could have called me to a place of failure.

Show me how You've spoken through my words. Let me see evidence that this calling was from You. Don't let me deceive myself either way. I'm at a place where what I desire most is Your truth.

There have been times when You've used my writing. I admit. But do those few times mean You meant me to *be* a writer? Clear out the confusion and replace it with the light of Your plan. Ensure that my heart's desire lines up with all that You have in store for me. I trust You, and I trust the fact that You love me. Use me where I am, and open my eyes to see You at work. Amen.

What Are We Afraid Of?

The fear of the Lord is a fountain of life, turning people away from the snares of death (Proverbs 14:27 HCSB).

We writers are a fearful lot.

We allow roadblocks to stand between us and the words we're called to share.

> The opinions of others.
> Being ridiculed.
> Falling short.
> Failing.
> Success.

And writers don't have a monopoly on fear. Everyone I know struggles against this deadly enemy. No, I didn't misspeak. Fear is deadly. It strangles all hope, kills all our dreams, whispers dreadful thoughts that paralyze us.

But what if fear isn't always a death sentence for our dreams. What if the right kind of fears could propel us into fulfilling our callings?

I'd like to propose that we can turn our fears on its head.

What if…

Instead of fearing the opinions of others, we feared the opinion of God

Instead of fearing ridicule, we feared NOT standing for something that matters.

Instead of fearing falling short, we feared not making an effort.

Instead of failing, we feared immobility.

Instead of fearing success, we feared putting emphasis on wrong ideals.

Today I'm starting new. I'm redirecting my feelings of fear in the right direction. How about you? What fear do you need to redirect to once again get back in the middle of the path God has for you?

Forging a
Creative Connection

*C*olors can have a powerful impact on our moods. In advertising, numerous studies have proven what colors are best to enhance the mood of what's being sold. Today I want you to choose a color that represents courage to you.

Here are the supplies you'll need:

- ☑ This book
- ☑ Pen or pencil
- ☑ Optional
- ☑ Colored Pencils, Markers and/or colors
- ☑ Stickers
- ☑ Washi Tape
- ☑ Scrap Paper (any type, even old magazines or advertising flyers)

☑ Glue Stick

Fill the next page with the color you've chosen. Use a combination of the supplies listed and be as messy and out of the box as you'd like.

As you finish up, use a pen (or stick on letters) to add a Bible verse that speaks to you about courage.

A Prayer Renaming Fear

Blessed is the man who trusts in the LORD, And whose hope is the LORD (Jeremiah 17:7 NKJV).

Dear Lord, You are my anchor in the storm that threatens to overwhelm me. Everywhere I turn I'm faced with fears that terrify me. Some of the fears I recognize; some are lurking just beyond recognition.

Bring all the ideas and issues that scare me into the light—into Your Light. I know that only then can I see them for what they are. Teach me to release the ones that are irrelevant, and turn the others upside down.

I let these terrors keep me from writing and following Your path. Today I want to change. More than anything I want to write without a cloud of fear looming over my head. Show me how.

Give me friends and other writers who will re-mind me that You didn't call me to a place of uncertainty and fear. Don't let me allow these fears to isolate me, instead give me the courage to reach out. Show me how to help others who are struggling as well.

I know that You have called me. Now show me how to live as one called, going forth boldly and obediently as I write for You. Amen.

Quit Writing from a Place of Fear and Find Joy

The LORD is my strength and my shield; my heart trusts in him, and he helps me. My heart leaps for joy, and with my song I praise him (Psalm 28:7 NIV).

A while back, I was having difficulties with a project. As I tried to figure out why, it dawned on me that instead of writing with courage and faith, I was writing from a place of fear.

No wonder the work was so difficult. The revelation stunned me. If there's one thing I pride myself on (and that should have been my first clue I was about to fall flat on my face), it's the thought that I'm not afraid of anything.

As I travel and speak to writers, one of the first things I share with them is how being courageous has helped me with my writing endeavors.

So what did I do to overcome this roadblock?

1. I took my fear to God in prayer. His word is clear on the fact that we're not supposed to fear. I acknowledged what I'd been doing and turned my fears over to Him.

2. I made a list detailing all my fears specifically. I didn't simply think about them in my mind. I put those fears on paper. Know what I discovered? Most of the things I was worried about looked pretty silly on paper.

3. I looked at the parts of the list that weren't silly and turned them upside down. For example: I was afraid someone I loved would misunderstand my motive. To turn it upside down I considered the possibility that someone God loved would see Him more clearly. Yes, what I was fearful about could happen, but after flipping my perspective, I decided it was worth the risk.

4. I gave myself permission to write from a place of courage. I turned away from those voices that warned about bad results. Instead, I spread my writing wings and soared

into the freedom of wordplay. I recaptured the joy of writing from my heart, exploring the whisperings of God in the depths of my soul. I rediscovered writing from a place of grace.

Today I'd like you to take a long and sensitive look at where you are with your writing. Ask yourself if you're writing from a place of grace or a place of fear.

Forging a
Creative Connection

This exercise is to help us build courage.
Here are the supplies you'll need:

- ☑ This book
- ☑ Pen or pencil
- ☑ Optional
- ☑ Ruler
- ☑ Colored Pencils, Markers and/or crayons
- ☑ Stickers
- ☑ Washi Tape

Often when we step outside our comfort zone, we face our gatekeeper voices. These voices may try to discourage us from moving on to something new. We may hear or be bombarded by thoughts like:

I'll never be able to learn that
People will laugh when they hear I'm trying that
I'll never be good enough to write that.

These voices can shut down our creativity and keep us locked inside walls of fear. Today we're tearing down the walls, plank by plank.

On the next page, draw a wall. This isn't an art test, just draw a square and add horizontal lines for planks. Now draw a line down the middle. In each plank, on the left side, write your fear. On the right side, ask God to show you how to overcome it, then write it on the plank next to the fear. Decorate the page with color and/or stickers.

Action step: Now choose one of your fears and *do* what your wrote to overcome it.

A Prayer for Courage

*Arise, for it is your task, and we are with you; be strong
and do it (Ezra 10:4 ESV).*

Dear Lord, You know what a wimp I am. At
times it seems like my first love isn't really writing'
it's thinking up reasons to be fearful about my writing. You didn't design me to be this way, and You certainly didn't call me to a life of fear.

I know Your plan for me is to walk confidently
on the path before me. Help me learn how to do
walk forward. Enlarge my courage and turn my focus
away from the what-ifs that clutter my mind.

Some days I wake up confident in what's to
come. But often even that confidence is misplaced—
focused on me and my ability instead of on You.
That's when I get into the most trouble. Don't let
me substitute self-confidence for confidence in You.

Remind me that I don't have to get it right for You to use my words for the benefit of others.

You take my most timid offerings and use them to further Your kingdom. I don't have to write perfectly, hear perfectly, or even follow perfectly. Perfection is Your job, obedience is mine.

You gave me a precious gift when You called me to write. Thank you for choosing to use me. Don't let me waste it by being afraid. Amen.

3 Scripture Prescriptions to Meet God Where You Are

F ew of us wouldn't go see a doctor when we're ill. But for some reason, when our souls are ailing, we often avoid seeking the recommendations of our heavenly physician. This list of Bible verses are what I like to term, *scripture prescriptions*.

I recommend you don't scan over these verses, but use the following pages to decorate and write out what God is saying to you through each of them.

I also urge you to copy them onto index cards and tape them around your home and car. The constant reminder that God has an answer to what is wrong can bring us the peace we're so desperately craving.

Be strong and courageous. Do not be afraid or terrified because of them, for the LORD your God goes with you; he will never leave you nor forsake you (Deuteronomy 31:6 NIV).

Wait for the LORD; Be strong and let your heart take courage; Yes, wait for the LORD (Psalm 27:14 NASB).

I have told you these things so that in Me you may have peace. You will have suffering in this world. Be courageous! I have conquered the world (John 16:33 HCSB).

Chapter Two

Defeating Doubt

Doubt can be crippling to a writer. Like fear, doubt comes bubbling up from deep inside of us. It can handicap us in ways that are obvious and ways that kill us from the inside out.

We face two major sources of doubt. The first comes from the voices that live in our heads. They accuse us, holding our less-than-perfect work up to ridicule in our minds and pointing out all the reasons we'll never be good enough. The second is the voice of the enemy. He also whispers ugly lies that grow into weeds of doubt. If we don't take care of these vicious plants—ripping them out by the roots—they'll strangle our creativity and drown out our words. But the enemy is crafty. He uses different voices to speak these lies. Sometimes you'll hear him in the voice of a well-meaning friend or relative. At other times, his voice will seem to come from a person of influence or from your mind. He's a master at speaking in first person and imitating my voice.

How do we defeat such a crippling obstacle? First we must recognize the subtle work of allowing doubt to creep in. Doubt, like fear, masquerades as rational and reasonable thoughts. Our only weapon is the powerful light of God's truth. When our doubts are exposed to His light of truth, they shrivel and die. Nothing evil, incomplete, or destructive can withstand the intense light of God.

The Calling of God

The Lord said to me, You have seen correctly, for I watch over My word to accomplish it (Jeremiah 1:12 HCSB).

Believers often speak of our personal calling. We long to know that special something that God has for us to accomplish within his kingdom. Sometimes we treat the search for our calling as a quest or even a treasure hunt. But truthfully, our calling is buried deep within us, something we're born with. It's not a discovery to be made but a desire and yearning to accept and grow into.

God has ordered all our days before we were born. He's set into motion the events in and around us to shape us into what He has for us. Everything we need has been accounted for and placed within our grasp *at the proper time.*

Accepting and discovering His will means stepping out in faith, trying what feels uncomfortable, even missing the boat. Trying and failing isn't failure when our hearts are focused on God. We must move forward, even when there is no certainty of success. Just as it's much harder to turn a parked car than one that's already moving, we must move in the direction of God's calling, embracing what He has arranged.

Most importantly, we must understand the essence of success from God's perspective. Our success is rooted and grounded in our obedience to Him. The success of our calling is His and His alone. We are only the instrument He's chosen.

When we write what He's put on our hearts, we release the writing back to Him in obedience, in whatever form that happens to be. The form may take the shape of an article, a devotion, a blog, a story, or a book. But we have the assurance that God will watch over those words and accomplish His perfect will.

Forging a
Creative Connection

Sometimes we defeat doubt when we connect more strongly with God and with His personal calling. Today we're going to place an imaginary phone call—to God. Instead of speaking, I want you to write the dialogue of a cell phone conversation with God.

Here are the supplies you'll need:

- ☑ This book
- ☑ Pen or pencil
- ☑ Optional
- ☑ Colored Pencils, Markers and/or crayons
- ☑ Stickers
- ☑ Washi Tape

On the next page I want you to write the dialogue of a cell phone call with God. You can include descriptions of sound only. You're on a cell phone, so you can't see the expression on His face or know what He's seeing.

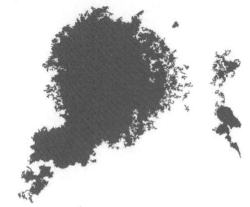

A Prayer Asking for God to Remind Me of My Calling

God will do this, for he is faithful to do what he says, and he has invited you into partnership with his Son, Jesus Christ our Lord (1 Corinthians 1:9 NLT).

Dear Lord, there was a time when I was certain of my call to write. I heard Your whisper deep in my soul, and then I felt the confirmation in the circumstances that followed. But I'm a long way from that call and even the echoes of it have faded away.

I confess that I now doubt whether or not I heard You correctly. Surely by now I'd have seen some fruit for all my effort. It seems so awful to say that, but it's the way I feel. I admit that part of me was hoping for more success, but I can honestly say I want that success to further Your kingdom and Your purpose.

Remind me of the writing successes because I've been obedient to You. I know there are times when You've used my words, but I can't recall anything. Maybe I should say I can't recall anything big.

That's the heart of it isn't it? I've been wanting something big, and You've been at work in the small things. I've made the mistake of judging small things to be worthless things. I know better than that. You care for the sparrow as much as for kings. But I'm so weary. Show me that You have a purpose for my puny efforts.

Give me a heart that's as strong and confident as the first day I heard You call. Dispel the doubt and return my joy as I serve You. Give me contentment where I am and a renewed sense of purpose as I continue to learn and grow as Your writer. Amen.

Am I Carrying Baggage or Luggage?

*Come to Me, all who are weary and heavy-laden, and
I will give you rest. Take My yoke upon you and learn
from Me, for I am gentle and humble in heart, and you
will find rest for your souls. For My yoke is easy and My
burden is light (Matthew 11:28-30 NASB).*

I don't know about you, but I have trouble letting
go of the past. I hold onto all my past writing and
publishing failures. The words may have even seemed
good at the time, but looking back I now know better.
I hoard those failures and let them feed my doubts
about how I'll do now and in the future.

Beyond holding onto the words I've written, I
hold onto interactions with other writers and pro-
fessionals—conversations and feelings that I'm not
proud of. I chew on past discussions and emails

where I wasn't a good example. All this holding on means I carry a lot of baggage that I don't need to. The baggage weighs down my soul and distracts me from the following God now.

All of these thoughts and internal weight can be boiled down into one thing. I'm doubting God's ability to cover my past mistakes and failures with His grace. I refuse to let go even though God has forgiven me.

At times, I add to this baggage with my refusal to forgive someone else for their interactions with me. I grasp the way they've hurt me and try to make it into some kind of armor against getting hurt again. But refusing to let go of the hurt someone else has caused is simply choosing to carry more baggage.

That kind of burden weighs a person down.

Baggage is something I need to get rid of to be a better—more obedient—writer. I must learn to drop it at the feet of Jesus and leave it there.

Luggage, on the other hand, is something that equips us for our travels. My luggage consists of the talents and abilities God has blessed me with. It also includes the lessons I've learned through the struggles and the triumphs of walking with God.

- The Bible verses I've memorized.
- The praise songs I've learned

- The stories about God's faithfulness.
- The writing that has impacted others.
- The writing that has impacted me.

Everyone needs some luggage to be equipped for the journey. The trick is to get rid of the baggage.

So today, begin evaluating whether the burden of doubt that's weighing down your writing is composed of baggage or luggage.

Forging a
Creative Connection

In today's devotion, we looked at the difference between baggage and luggage. All that thought about travel makes me want to get my journal make a list of what to pack. So that's what we're going to do.

Here are the supplies you'll need:

- ☑ This book
- ☑ Pen or pencil
- ☑ Optional
- ☑ Colored Pencils, Markers and/or crayons
- ☑ Stickers
- ☑ Washi Tape

At the top of the next page record a writing goal or dream. It can be big or small, just somewhere you really want to go with your writing . For example, it might be, *have a book in the bookstore*, or *get published in a national magazine.*

Now I want you to make a packing list of what you'll need to arrive at that destination. Here are some generic ideas:

- Bible verses that inspire you
- A writing conference
- Time to write
- Talent (be specific and name what talent)

You get the idea. Once you have your list, I want you to highlight the talents, gifts, and abilities God has already put in place to help you reach that goal. Finish with a short prayer thanking Him and asking for any additional help you need.

A Prayer to Lighten My Load

The LORD sustains all who fall And raises up all who are bowed down (Psalm 145:14 NASB).

Dear Lord, I know I'm carrying a lot of extra weight. I'm holding on to baggage that isn't mine to carry, and it's weighing me down and keeping me from following You. It clutters my mind keeping me from clarity and peace.

I know I'm hanging onto remarks others have made about my ability. They aren't from You, but because they were supposed to help me improve, I gave them credence. Why do I always cling to the negative? Why can't I give the good stuff I hear as much heed?

It's not only the bad advice I'm refusing to set down, it's the hurt that came with those words. I can call to mind the ugly memories so much quicker than Your words and what You have said about me.

Change that inclination. Show me how to cling to Your truth and to the good words spoken by those who listen to You.

Give me the discernment to know what I should listen to and keep with me and what I need to discard. Equip me to be a wise traveler, packing light and getting rid of the baggage I don't need. Amen.

A Writing Cross Road

Then Jesus said to his disciples, If any of you want to be my followers, you must forget about yourself. You must take up your cross and follow me. If you want to save your life, you will destroy it. But if you give up your life for me, you will find it (Matthew 16:24-25 CEV).

Take my life and let it be, consecrated all to Thee." The words to that old hymn recently transported me back in time. Many years ago, I hit a crossroad with God. I knew He'd called me to write—in my heart I knew—but all around me everything was rejection and heartache. I'd been so thrilled when God whispered that calling. It felt . . . right. I'd barely heard the words when I began mapping out my future. I knew He'd want me to write Bible studies and teach and speak—bringing His Word to His people. My vision was full of me and how I'd impact His kingdom. But looking back I can see I was focused on my glory, not His.

Then came the struggle. And finally that night when my dream, and what I thought God had promised, lay in shattered pieces around me. I spoke my frustration to God that dark evening out loud, and shook a metaphorical fist toward Heaven. "I didn't ask for this gift of writing—this insane compulsion. Why make me suffer for it?"

Even before the echo of my cry died away I knew it for the lie it was. I remembered an earlier time in my life, when I'd committed myself to God, asking Him to do what He willed with my life. And now I complained because He had? I'd known what that commitment meant and the suffering that would come. How could I have ever thought suffering would be easy or martyrdom pleasant?

That night at the crossroad, I surrendered to a different writing future. My new future was one where I didn't second guess God's plan, but kept my gaze locked tightly on Him. I chose to trust Him and believe that He knew what was best for me, no matter what.

That was the night I died—died to myself and my own dreams of glory—and began to learn how to live for Him. It was when I learned that to be truly His in *every way* means giving up my *every way*.

I didn't know if God would resurrect me as a writer. Only time held that answer, but I had to come to a point where I committed to His will—even for my writing. Did I care? Oh I cared; I desperately cared. My dreams, my hopes, my ambitions had been tied to my writing. But I was making the decision to turn all of that over. From that point on, I vowed that I'd do my very best to turn my ambition into emptying myself so that I could be filled with God.

I changed my wish from *God to make me look good because I work for You* to *make me look any way You choose because I'm totally Yours.*

It was a true Cross Road.

So how has that worked out? The story isn't finished, but many years have passed since that dark night. The journey hasn't been easy, and my publishing career doesn't look much like I originally imagined. My life hasn't taken the path I thought—it's taken one that's been infinitely richer than I could have ever imagined.

God has taken me places—physically and spiritually—I wouldn't have dared to dream about, and I dreamed some pretty big stuff. *Only* He could have accomplished so much.

Many of you are where I was—second guessing your calling because it doesn't look like what you thought it would. I urge you to stay the course. Place your confidence in a Worthy God.

Forging a
Creative Connection

Sometimes we must make hard choices to follow God. A writer's life is full of choices. Do I write or do I .... Sometimes the answer is writing, sometimes it's something else. But those choices are easier if we're prepared in advance to make them. So we're going to practice.

Here are the supplies you'll need:

- ☑ This book
- ☑ Pen or pencil
- ☑ Optional
- ☑ Colored Pencils, Markers and/or crayons
- ☑ Stickers
- ☑ Washi Tape

I want you to come up with a list of all you're willing to give up to write. But there's a catch. You can only use the letters from this phrase: Write your list on the next page.

Moving Past the Writers Cross Road

After you've finished with your list, decorate it and add a Bible verse that means something to you as a writer.

A Prayer to Move Forward

*Surely the Sovereign LORD does nothing without revealing his plan to his servants the prophets
(Amos 3:7 NIV).*

Dear Lord, I find myself at a decision point in my writing life. I heard Your call and began this journey. I felt like I had a clear vision of where we were headed. But although I see the goal, it might as well be a million miles away. There are too many obstacles between me and where I thought You wanted me to go. Show me where I've gone wrong. I'm ready to stop striving and listen to what You have for me.

I feel like I've been wandering in the wilderness and unable to make any progress. Today I'm asking for clarification. I need to know that all the time I've spent hasn't been wasted. Give me concrete examples of how You've used this journey.

I had such high hopes and none of them have come to pass. Show me where I need to readjust my expectations. I'm tired of being so focused on what I thought was my destination, that I've lost sight of You. I haven't meant to drift away from You, but every time I try to make forward progress, I end up leaving Your side.

Help me understand what's happening. Empty me of my expectations—and even my dreams. Give me a clear vision of how to walk with You through this writing journey. Amen.

Accepting the Post of Ambassador

Therefore, we are ambassadors for Christ, certain that God is appealing through us (2 Corinthians 5:20 HCSB).

I'm constantly amazed at how God chooses to use me in His work. It's humbling and terrifying at the same time.

I've been looking at this verse, trying to wrap my mind around understanding how to be an *ambassador for Christ* when it's applied to the life of a writer. As I've studied the parallels between the role of ambassadors in world governments and our role as Christ-following-writers, I found lessons hidden there.

Ambassadors don't live in their home countries. They are strangers in a strange land. That description is also true of believers. This world is our temporary home, even though our time here can sometimes seems endless.

Ambassadors are appointed, not elected. They haven't campaigned for their position; it's a gift of responsibility. We are also appointed—as believers and as writers for the kingdom—chosen by God and elevated to the position of spiritual ambassador. It's not because we're better than anyone else, it's simply a gift of grace.

Ambassadors don't get to choose their country of service. That too is the choice of the one they serve. As writers, we have each been chosen to serve where God places us. He's the one who brings the words, the contracts, and the publication.

As a writer, I've often chaffed at this restriction. I wanted to do big things for God. I had a definite opinion about where and how I wanted to live out my dream.

Thank goodness God had other plans.

It turns out, when I look back, His plans were much better. They went farther and deeper than I ever imagined. For some reason, we writers tend to think too small. And we insist that God follows our way, the outcome will be a shadow of what we want. But in His plan, we will be astonished.

Forging a Creative Connection

With this activity, we're going to practice being ambassadors. Often we get caught in the trap of wanting to do big things for God and bring attention to what He's doing. But there is great value—and perspective—in blessing someone else.

Here are the supplies you'll need:

- ☑ This book
- ☑ Notecard
- ☑ Pen or pencil
- ☑ Optional
- ☑ Colored Pencils, Markers and/or crayons
- ☑ Stickers
- ☑ Washi Tape

Today we're going to visit a strange land, a bookstore. I know that seems like familiar territory; it is, and it isn't. If you can't make it to a physical bookstore, get ready to browse some online shelves. Or a trip to your local library will work just as well.

Pick out a book that has left an impression on you. Now write a thank you note to the author. In your thank you note, be sure to let them know you're praying for them. If possible find their address or the address of their publisher and mail it to them. If not send them (or their publisher) an email. Now go one step further and post a review of the book, recommending it to your social media community.

A Prayer for a Stranger in a Strange Land

*For this world is not our permanent home; we are looking forward to a home yet to come
(Hebrews 13:14 NLT).*

Dear Lord, every day I'm reminded that I live in a place that isn't my home. This world becomes more and more strange as it drifts farther from Your truth. I often wonder how a writer who follows You can have any impact in such an evil time as this.

I know Your Word tells us that the world hated You and it will hate those who belong to You, but somehow I didn't expect it to hurt so much. I'm weary of writing to a culture that has nothing but contempt for You, as they celebrate ideas and actions that bring You sorrow and ridicule the truth You hold dear.

I thought when I agreed to write for You that I'd be writing to those who know You. I'd encourage my brothers and sisters, and lead those eager to know You into a deeper relationship. Instead You've sent me into places where people hate You. You've asked me to stand up for You on social media and through all sorts of uncomfortable situations.

You've asked me to learn about technology that scares me and reach out to people who already hate me. I'm such a coward at heart, and I need Your courage as I continue.

Surround me with other believers who can encourage me. Use us to strengthen one another as we go into the world bearing a light it's determined to extinguish. Keep me strong and focused on You, no matter what. Amen.

Time to Refocus My Life

You do not want a sacrifice, or I would give it; You are not pleased with a burnt offering. (Psalm 51:16 HCSB).

I don't know about you, but I'm a doer. No matter how hard I try, I can't seem to help myself. And while I have made some improvement over the years, unless I'm really focused, I'm going to judge my day, my progress, even *my worth*, on the jobs I've accomplished. This overachieving fixation is especially true in my writing.

I know in my head that a check mark by every listing on my to-do list isn't synonymous for my significance. Unfortunately, I can't seem to get my feelings to switch over to this way of thinking. This unhealthy outlook permeates every part of my life, especially spiritually. I keep acting as if I can win God's favor by doing more.

There was a time in my writing life when I was working seven days a week. I was writing blogs, publishing articles, writing and submitting manuscripts to be turned into books, etc. I was a busy bee for God's kingdom. But my busyness had changed my focus of being with God to doing things for God. Inevitably that kind of pace and focus ended with me in a pile of exhaustion and chaos.

And that was when I admitted to God that it was time to refocus my life.

From my collapse, God rebuilt me from the ground up. He showed me that being a Christ-follower has its emphasis on the state of being verb, rather than an action verb.

God has always been more interested in the process rather than the product.

I came to understand that God is relational, not task, oriented. Whatever needs doing, He can do. He uses us to accomplish His will—not to keep us busy or because He doesn't have the time. He allows us to join Him where He's working because of the relationship between us.

God wants to spend time with me. He wants me to be so familiar with His voice that I can instantly hear and respond when He calls my name. But when I fill my life with my to-do list, my focus drifts. Tasks capture my attention and draw me away from the relationship.

So I've learned to be constantly adjusting the focus on my life. I'm looking at the person of God and making sure my plans include spending more time with Him, instead of for Him.

Forging a Creative Connection

Today we're going to practice two things, focusing and state of being.

Here are the supplies you'll need:

- ☑ This book
- ☑ Pen or pencil
- ☑ Camera (cell phone or regular camera)
- ☑ Optional
- ☑ Colored Pencils, Markers and/or crayons
- ☑ Stickers
- ☑ Washi Tape

Go outside, and take a seat. If you can get to a park or out in nature, that's ideal. Otherwise find a place where you can see natural things like a plant or even insects. As you settle into your seat, take a few deep breaths and try to calm your mind. Say a short prayer asking God to open your eyes.

Now observe what going on around you. Focus on whatever draws your attention, a leaf, blade of grass, insect or bird. Next use your camera to get an even narrower focus by observing your subject through the camera lens. Snap a couple of pictures. Notice the movement, the colors, the sounds. Ask God to speak to you through your observations. Record what He says on the next page.

A Prayer to Readjust My Focus

But seek first the kingdom of God and His righteousness ,and all these things will be provided for you (Matthew 6:33 HCSB).

Dear Lord, once again I've gotten upside down in my priorities. I'm spending more time doing *for* You, than time *with* you. I've run ahead and now I have trouble finding You in the midst of my busyness.

Now I'm exhausted and frustrated because all my activity seems futile, bearing no fruit. Why should it when You're not part of it? I've been filled with doubt because of the emptiness, and it's my own fault.

Forgive me for never seeming to learn this lesson. Help me build some checks and balances that show me when my focus drifts. All of this busyness is worthless without You.

I need some accountability with other writers who understand this business and can help me make wiser choices. Please send a few friends to me and give me a group that encourages one another even as we help each other stay on track.

Remake my schedule and help me shed everything You didn't have for me in the first place. Get me out of the way so Your purpose is once again front and center. Keep me close to You and help me always stay focused on You and You alone. Amen.

3 Scripture Prescriptions to Meet God Where You Are

There are very few of us who wouldn't go see a doctor when we're ill. But for some reason, when our souls are ailing, we often avoid seeking out the recommendations of our heavenly physician. This list of Bible verses are what I like to term, *scripture prescriptions*.

I recommend you don't simply scan them, but use the following pages to decorate and write out what God is saying to you through each of them.

I also urge you to copy them onto index cards and tape them around your home and car. The constant reminder that God has an answer to what is wrong can bring us the peace we're so desperately craving.

But Jesus said, "Why are you so frightened? Why do you doubt? (Luke 24:38 CEV).

But when you ask, you must believe and not doubt, because the one who doubts is like a wave of the sea, blown and tossed by the wind (James 1:6 NIV).

Do not fear, for I am with you; Do not anxiously look about you, for I am your God. I will strengthen you, surely I will help you, Surely I will uphold you with My righteous right hand (Isaiah 41:10 NASB).

Chapter Three

Banishing Blocks

All writers face writer's block. Some writers call this phenomena by different names, but everyone goes through times—and even seasons—when they struggle with creativity. Sometimes it's weariness that drains the well dry. At other times it's failure. And I've known many writers that have experienced blocks because of success.

Whatever the reason, we have to find ways of dealing with a shortage of creativity and motivation. Fortunately, we serve a God of infinite reserves and plenty of creativity to go around. He's generous with inspiration and never short of grace when we're the problem behind the blocks.

His antidotes for writer's block never comes with condemnation. It's delivered with the soft voice that speaks to us of His calling and is seasoned with love. He equips us in the season of plenty and the season of drought. Draw deeply from His well and learn what it means to write with a God of infinite reserves.

Am I Letting the Past Keep Me From the Future?

My friends, I don't feel that I have already arrived. But I forget what is behind, and I struggle for what is ahead. I run toward the goal, so that I can win the prize of being called to heaven. This is the prize that God offers because of what Christ Jesus has done
(Philippians 3:13-14 CEV).

Publishing is a tough business.

It's almost impossible to write anything for public consumption without feeling like you're throwing your heart into the lion's den. And I don't know about you, but I give negative comments a lot more credibility than the positive ones. The good ones I tend to disregard with the thought that the person commenting was *just being nice.*

Past rejections make it possible to shrivel up and die, at least as a writer. Feeding ourselves on what's gone before forces us to a standstill. It's easy to become overwhelmed with doubt, insecurity, and an almost overwhelming urge to give up.

Instead, we need to fill our minds with the affirmation that God sends our way.

I have two dusty scraps of paper that hang above my desk. One is from a critique partner. At the bottom of one of my pages she wrote several sentences, one of which told me she could see God in my writing. The other scrap is part of a note I received from one of my readers.

God sent me both of those messages when I was at a low point. He used them to renew my hope and assure me that He was using my words to touch others.

As writers, we must be careful who we let speak truth into our lives. If we give the enemy the power to tell us lies, we'll find ourselves blocked and ineffective.

Instead, draw a line in the sand. Commit today, right now, to begin to live in the future, on the promises God has given you.

If you're writing now, you know what I mean. You've heard that still, small voice call your name. You've gotten that confirmation you've asked for.

Now it's time to move forward, believing God truly is big enough to make it happen. He doesn't call us out, fully formed and ready. He calls us out when we're weak—ready for Him to equip us.

Forging a
Creative Connection

I've discovered there's no time like the present to get rid of the past.

Here are the supplies you'll need:

- ☑ This book
- ☑ Pen or pencil
- ☑ Several sheets of paper
- ☑ Envelope
- ☑ Matches

Some place you can safely light a small fire—even a candle will work in a pinch

Optional

    ☑ Colored Pencils, Markers and/or crayons

    ☑ Stickers

    ☑ Washi Tape

I want you to think about all the negative words that have been said to you, or thoughts you've believed about yourself that have hampered your writing. Write each one on the paper. Be as specific as possible. As you write each, ask God to release you from the falsehoods in that negative statement.

Tear the paper into tiny pieces and set them on fire. Make a commitment to God that you will remember those lies no longer.

In our journal, write your feelings about what you just did.

A Prayer to Recalibrate My Memory

Let all that I am praise the LORD; may I never forget the good things he does for me (Psalm 103:2 NLT).

Dear Lord, I have a memory problem. I remember negatives that I shouldn't and forget positives that I should. Right now I can recall almost every negative remark ever said about my writing. Yet I have trouble remembering good comments.

Beyond that, my memory tends to rewrite history. It inflates and exaggerates the negative and minimizes the positive. I'm struggling to stay motivated and engaged because of this memory problem.

You are Lord of all—even my crazy thoughts. I know that You and You alone are able to help me. I need Your perspective and wisdom. I want to know honestly where I need to improve, but I also need to know what, and if, there's anything good about the sentences and paragraphs I write.

I remember when I felt Your call to write. Assure me I didn't imagine it or turn my selfish desires into a command from You. Help me recalibrate my faulty memory and sort out truth from fiction.

Sort through my mind and give me Your insight. I want to follow Your path with my writing, and I can only do that with Your illuminating truth. Amen.

Thoughts on Being a Submissive Writer

Submit yourselves, then, to God. Resist the devil, and he will flee from you (James 4:7 NIV).

As writers, we're constantly being called to submit, even if we don't realize it. Of course there's the obvious connection, when we submit our writing for possible publication. But there are other ways as well.

We submit to God's call when we put our words in tangible form—either handwritten or in a digital document.

We submit to others when we share our words for critique.

We submit when we invest our time and energy in organizations, classes, and conferences.

These acts of submission are part of the path we must follow to become a working writer. This process is sometimes painful, but growth and obedience always are.

Submission is also an act that can bring on spiritual warfare.

When we turn from the ourselves and the world, taking that first step to follow God in obedience, we invite attack from the enemy. We can expect him to come after us.

He tries to fill our days with busyness—often camouflaging it with good works to tempt us away from God's best.

He will use others to bring us down with negative words.

He whispers into our minds, saying we inadequate and bad.

He tries to make us doubt what God has shown us.

But James says that submission empowers us. When we refuse to be drawn off God's path, Satan will flee. Maybe he won't disappear forever, but by submitting we have a powerful weapon to combat him.

Forging a
Creative Connection

*S*ubmission is difficult for most of us. It takes practice and diligence to lead a life submitted to God. This exercise will help us be more diligent about submission.

Here are the supplies you'll need:

- ☑ This book
- ☑ Pen or pencil
- ☑ Optional
- ☑ Colored Pencils, Markers and/or crayons
- ☑ Stickers
- ☑ Washi Tape

We're going to write a prayer statement to God about being submissive using the letters of the word:

S U B M I T

You may use each letter as the first letter of a word, or a letter within the word. You can also use more than one word per letter if you wish.

Here's an example of one I did with the word PEACE

> **P**erfect
>
> **E**ase
>
> **A**ccepting
>
> **C**hrist's
>
> **E**quipping

A Prayer As I Learn to Submit

Submit to God, and you will have peace; then things will go well for you (Job 22:21 NLT).

Dear Lord, I'm struggling in many aspects of my writing. Where once I looked forward to putting words on paper, now I can come up with hundreds of excuses instead of writing. I avoid my writers group, and when I attend I come away empty handed. And actually submitting something to a publishing professional is so far from my mind, I wonder if I ever will.

I love to write. What's wrong with me? I know there's got to be something else going on here. Truthfully, I suspect that I have a submission problem. Most of what I'm struggling with is an unwillingness to submit to Your call.

There are other priorities in my life, but I've let my fear feed my disobedience, and I've neglected Your will when it comes to writing. Help me find the strength to sit in my chair, place my fingers on the keyboard and write.

I want what I write to bring You joy. In striving for perfection, I've quit trying. I've let my wants and needs overshadow the obedience You ask of me. Help me let go of all the obstacles that stand between me and the path You have before me. Remake me into a submissive writer who writes in obedience and leaves the results to You. Amen.

Expectations as a Stumbling Block

My soul, wait in silence for God only, For my hope is from Him (Psalm 62:5 NIV).

When I was young all I wanted to be was a writer. As a matter of fact, I actually wrote my first novel in eighth grade...long hand, with a purple ink pen. But through the years, my dream of writing drifted farther and farther from the realm of reasonable possibilities, until I finally I gave up.

But as a young mother of three kids, God revived that call. At first I was scared, but then I got excited. Oh the plans I made—I'd write Bible studies and spend my time traveling, speaking, and working for God.

I finished my first Bible study and the printer ink was barely dry before I had the manuscript in an envelope and on the way to publisher. I could see my future so clearly, and I was on fire with plans to do great feats in His kingdom. All He had to do was open this one door.

Not only did He *not* open that door, it seemed every other door had slammed shut and locked. It quickly became obvious that *going* and doing weren't part of His call to me. Instead, the doors at home began to swing wide, as He invited me to share my story with those closest to me.

As I swallowed my pride and became obedient to act where He'd placed me, the fruit began to grow. Years later, going and doing has become part of my call, but first I'd had to learn obedience and the difference between His will and mine.

Forging a
Creative Connection

*L*earning to embrace the now. Every moment of everyday is unique for each of us. Even if we're all in the same room, watching the same television show, our perspective is slightly different, our attitude, and our experiences are different.

Here are the supplies you'll need:

- ☑ This book
- ☑ Pen or pencil
- ☑ Optional
- ☑ Colored Pencils, Markers and/or crayons
- ☑ Stickers
- ☑ Washi Tape

Draw or trace a large circle on the next page. Find a quiet corner and set a timer for sixty seconds. Before you start the timer, say a prayer and ask God to speak to you. During that short time period, pay close attention to what's happening around you.

When the sixty seconds is up, record what you experienced in the circle you drew. Use your five senses to help you recall everything you can from that one short minute. Now, outside the circle, brainstorm ways you could write about what you experienced.

A Prayer About Expectations

For I am confident of this very thing, that He who began a good work in you will perfect it until the day of Christ Jesus (Philippians 1:6 NASB).

Dear Lord, I had such energy and hope when I first heard you whisper that I would be a writer. My imagination and dreams soared to the apex of what that calling could be. But now I'm no longer flying, instead I'm crawling through the mud of defeat and despair. Every word I write feels stale and like it's all been said before. Am I faithfully following Your call or should I just give up

Help me let go of my own expectations and be a conduit for Your words. I want to share Your love through the words You have for me to write. Replace the false voices with the calling that allows me to be exactly who You made me to be.

Speak to me. Let me clearly hear Your plan for my life. Lead me into fresh ways to write about You. Fill my sentences with words that touch the minds and hearts of those who read them. Let me see the world around me with fresh eyes as You speak Your truth in unusual ways. Then guide my hands as I record what You've shown me.

Your world is a place of color and texture; sounds and smells. Renew my ability to paint pictures with words. Fill me with Your Spirit as my fingers once again fly across the keyboard. You are my inspiration and my joy. Open a pathway for that joy to spill over into my words as I write. Amen.

Out of the Fog and Into the Sun

Faithful is He who calls you, and He also will bring it to pass (1 Thessalonians 5:24 HCSB).

Many of you know I have a special place in my heart for the Blue Ridge Mountains Christian Writers Conference. I'm privileged to be one of the directors of this wonderful conference, and it's always a highlight of my writing year.

But I didn't start out on staff—far from it.

I started as a nervous, first-time attendee who wondered if she'd heard God right when He called. It's a daunting prospect to take your dreams out of the clouds and into real life. And that's what you're doing if you've attended a writers conference.

I remember one year, I got up before dawn to make the drive to the conference. As I wound my way toward the mountains, God surprised me with a glorious sunrise reflecting off the clouds. Everything about it held the promise of great things to come.

But as I got closer to my goal in the mountains, the clouds descended and fog engulfed my car. I was forced to slow—almost to a crawl at times—because the fog was so thick. As I drove I thought of my writing journey.

It began with a glorious revelation from God. He gifted me with an idea and the tools to pursue my dream. He even arranged for me to speak at my first women's retreat—all within a few months of my decision to dedicate my writing to him.

But then the clouds descended. I couldn't get any traction at all. Everything in the universe, from friends to family to finances seemed determined to keep me from my goal. It got so bad, I began to wonder if I'd somehow gotten off on the wrong track.

Looking back at those dark years, before publication, I can see God was growing me. He was honing his instrument, testing my readiness, giving me the foundation I had to have to stay the course.

Just like my trip to the mountains, the writer's path can be filled with unexpected clouds. When I drove into the fog, I didn't stop and camp there. I kept going. I knew the goal lay before me, even if it was currently out of sight.

There are going to be times during this journey when we'll feel like we've ended up in a fog bank. God, just like the sun, can seem to be blocked by clouds of confusion and doubt. At those times, we need to remember our goals and keep climbing. As long as we keep moving, the sun will shine again.

Forging a
Creative Connection

Today we're going to chase the light. If it's a sunny day, you're in for a treat. If it's overcast, you're going to have to work a little bit harder (or put this exercise off until a sunny day).

Here are the supplies you'll need:

- ☑ This book
- ☑ Pen or pencil
- ☑ Cell phone camera or regular camera
- ☑ Optional
- ☑ Sketch book if you prefer that to a camera
- ☑ Colored Pencils, Markers and/or crayons
- ☑ Stickers
- ☑ Washi Tape

The writing journey can be littered with cloudy, dreary days. During those times, we must be diligent to look for the God-moments that bring flashes of light and inspiration.

Today's assignment is a photo scavenger hunt. You may have to do some hunting to find all of these, but the challenge will energize your creative muscles. Once you have your images, ask God to help you choose one of them to write about on the next page. It could be a scene, a made up story, a poem, whatever you wish. Thank God for the opportunity to see something new and write about it.

Here's what to search for and snap a picture of (or sketch)

- ☑ Steam rising from a hot beverage
- ☑ New growth on a tree or a plant
- ☑ A crosswalk with people in it
- ☑ A puppy
- ☑ A reflection in water
- ☑ An old piece of jewelry
- ☑ Shadows on pavement

A Prayer for the Sun to Shine Again

But if from there you seek the Lord your God, you will find him if you seek him with all your heart and with all your soul (Deuteronomy 4:29 NIV).

Dear Lord, I began this writing journey with such joy. I knew I was following Your path and I could see Your purpose so clearly in what I was doing. But lately I've found myself surrounded by a thick fog. It's hard for me to see the next step because everything is so unclear.

I look up, hoping to see the direction of Your light, but everything seems gray. Help me make my way out of this cloud. I want to once again experience the warm light of walking close to You as I follow my dreams.

My first reaction has been to stop and wait on the light to once again appear. But I know I need to continue on in obedience. Keep me from losing heart and coming to a complete stop.

Give me confirmation that I'm still on the right track. Remind me that You haven't moved. You're still in control and even when I can't sense it, You still walk with me. As I look around, renew my wonder of finding You in the little places. Let me see You in the ray of sun reflecting off the water or the curl of steam rising my morning cup of tea. You aren't just a God of majestic moments, You are present in the smallest detail.

Surround me with others who will be my encouragement on this journey. It's so much easier to travel a difficult journey with friends. Lead me to others who are intent on following Your path. Fill my life with other writers and allow us to spur each other on as we follow You. Amen.

The Word of My Testimony

They conquered him by the blood of the Lamb and by the word of their testimony, for they did not love their lives in the face of death (Revelation 12:11 HCSB).

Once again I found myself facing a video camera and being interviewed about being a writer.

"What do you find hardest about being a writer?"

Situations like this, was the answer on the tip of my tongue.

Fortunately I had prayed for God to put a guard over my tongue, and I managed to stammer out a less revealing answer.

I absolutely hate being interviewed with me as the focus. You see, I'm a background sort of girl, and any kind of attention makes me desperately uncomfortable. And, in my mind, I've always thought that was the way it should be. I'm only where I am because of God's blessings—not anything I've done. So situations that bring attention on me seem to diametrically opposed to bringing glory to God.

Then one day I was told differently.

Who dared to argue with my supposed biblical point of view? Someone whose authority I couldn't fight—God.

It was the verse in Revelation 12:11 that is printed above that stopped me in my tracks.

There it was, one powerful word—*testimony*—that word caused me a death of sorts. The death of my quiet, comfortable, life-in-the-shadows life. You see, my testimony is what God has done in my life. And God wants to use my story to defeat the enemy.

Have you ever tried to share a personal testimony without talking about yourself? Don't bother trying—trust me. It's not possible.

So what am I going to do with this information? The only thing I can do—try to be obedient—no matter how uncomfortable it makes me. Because the one thing I know is that this life isn't about me.

Forging a Creative Connection

*S*haring what God has done and what He's currently doing through our writing feels an awful lot like bragging. However, as we learned in today's devotion, God uses our personal experiences with Him to defeat the enemy. But we can't share something we don't know. Today's task is going to involve some soul searching.

Here are the supplies you'll need:

- ☑ This book
- ☑ Pen or pencil
- ☑ Optional
- ☑ Colored Pencils, Markers and/or crayons
- ☑ Stickers
- ☑ Washi Tape

On the next page write a heading: What God Has Done

Now make a list of moments when God has worked in and through your life. This page is private, and I'm not going to ask you to share it with anyone, so be totally open, honest, and transparent. Luxuriate in the fullness of how God has used you in His work. As you make the list, whisper prayers of thanksgiving and feel His joy in you—His obedient child.

292 9781946708366 292

Location: B2

VOM.PH

Title: Soul Care for Writers
Cond: Good
User: vo_list
Station: DESKTOP-95EUL5F
Date: 2020-03-19 20:18:42 (UTC)
Account: Veteran-Outsource
Orig Loc: B2
mSKU: VOM.PH
Seq#:   292
QuickPick   5RM
unit_id: 193359
width.   0.58 in

delist unit# 193359

xxxxx

A Prayer for Boldness

He proclaimed the kingdom of God and taught about the Lord Jesus Christ—with all boldness and without hindrance! (Acts 28:31 NIV).

Dear Lord, You are a God of courage and boldness. You lead Your followers into victories that cannot be imagined. So why am I so timid and fearful when it comes to speaking about You?

At first, it seemed that my reticence stemmed from a desire to be humble, but now I'm not so sure my attitude is fully accurate. I know I would be nothing without You, but you've been so active in my life. So I'm struggling with how to share all those amazing moments without mentioning me.

I want everyone to know the powerful ways You're working in my life. At the same time, I don't want to call attention to myself. It's a difficult tightrope to walk, and I need Your guidance.

Give me boldness without fear when I speak of You. Don't let inaccurate comments from others lead me to be silent about You.

Show me how to share Your work and Your presence in my life without bragging about me. Keep me from any false humility that doesn't honor You. Most of all don't ever let me believe that any of my success stems from me. Amen.

3 Scripture Prescriptions to Meet God Where You Are

There are very few of us who wouldn't go see a doctor when we're ill. But for some reason, when our souls are ailing, we often avoid seeking out the recommendations of our heavenly physician. This list of Bible verses are what I like to term, *scripture prescriptions*.

I recommend you don't simply scan them, but use the following pages to decorate and write out what God is teaching you through each of them.

I also urge you to copy them onto index cards and tape them around your home and car. The constant reminder that God has an answer to what is wrong can bring us the peace we're so desperately craving.

For the LORD your God is the One who goes with you to fight for you against your enemies to give you victory (Deuteronomy 20:4 HCSB).

For I know the plans I have for you, declares the LORD, plans to prosper you and not to harm you, plans to give you hope and a future (Jeremiah 29:11 NIV).

No, in all these things we are more than victorious through Him who loved us. (Romans 8:37 HCSB),

Chapter Four

Conquering Comparisons

Writers love comparisons. We use them as a tool in our writing, but we also use them to gage where we stand. We compare ourselves to other writers—the best sellers and the no sellers, the slightly ahead and the slightly behind, the full-timers and the hobbyists—and we compare ourselves to ourselves.

The snare of judging our worth against others can prove to be a major downfall for many of us. Yes, evaluating our progress on the writing journey is often a healthy way to set goals and keep track of our progress. But judgment is subjective, and when we pay too much attention to comparisons, it can halt all forward momentum.

We must learn to use comparison as a tool and avoid it when it becomes a trap. Each of us has a unique path as a writer. What is success for one, might be failure for another. Only through God's eyes can we get an accurate measure of where we are and whether or not we're in the center of His will. Together we'll explore how to put some healthy guards in place to ensure our journey is snare free.

Writing Without a Filter

Therefore, having put away falsehood, let each one of you speak the truth with his neighbor, for we are members one of another (Ephesians 4:15 ESV).

I'm a photographer and love all the creative things I can do in post-editing with the images I take. When I first began experimenting with my photos, I got a little wild with all the different effects. By adding different filters, I could completely change the look of a picture.

Where once an image was sunny and bright, I could bring it down to look dark and gloomy. I could also do the opposite. I added frames, embedded graphics, even melded two images into one. The options were endless.

But once the new wore off all these editing tricks, I found that my favorite images were the ones that looked most like real life—with little or no effects applied. The photos that captured the moment I had experienced, without embellishment, brought me the most joy. Those unadorned pictures were also the ones that garnered the most attention when I showed them to others. They seemed to bring out the best conversations.

And not too long ago, God whispered a parallel truth to me about my life. So often, when I speak about me—especially in regard to my writing—my tendency is to apply a filter. It doesn't matter if it's something positive or negative, I can't seem to simply lay it out there. I play around with what I share, how I share it, and even the spin I put on it when I share it.

I try to frame my experiences and embellish them with explanations and logic. I apologize for the good things, downplay the negative things, and generally try to neaten life up.

But the times when I'm most honest about what I'm experiencing, are the times when I connect deepest with those around me. Those moments of transparency and realism are when God can come in and touch others. It's when I'm most vulnerable, that I'm most valuable to the kingdom.

Forging a Creative Connection

We view life through many types of filters. Experiences, expectations, and attitude are just a few. The trick is to get rid of the filters that hinder God's work in and through us. Today we're going to play with some filters and ways they obstruct our view.

Here are the supplies you'll need:

- ☑ This book
- ☑ Pen or pencil
- ☑ A filmy scarf or thin piece of fabric.
- ☑ Optional
- ☑ Colored Pencils, Markers and/or crayons
- ☑ Stickers
- ☑ Washi Tape

Begin by draping the fabric over your head so it covers your eyes, nose, and mouth. To get the full effect, you should still be able to see through it a little bit. Now go into a room or area that you're familiar with. Find a seat and observe how different the room is when viewed through your filter.

Use the next page to write about the colors you see and anything that strikes you about the experience. Notice how the filter affects all your senses.

Now remove the filter and write your perceptions of the room unfiltered. Ask God to share His insight into the filters

A Prayer for Honesty

Whoever walks in integrity walks securely, but whoever
takes crooked paths will be found out
(Proverbs 10:9 NIV).

Dear Lord, I always want to be honest, but some of the things I feel You asking me to share are uncomfortable. When what I write leaves my hands, I know I don't have any control over where it will land. I can't know if it will be read by someone who understands, or who assigns the worst possible motives to what I write.

I shouldn't be worried about how I look to others, but I confess that I do. I don't want someone to be kept from You because of something wrote. Beyond that, some writing might impact those I love.

Knowing exactly what to share in every circumstance is a minefield of potential explosions. Help me navigate the path. Don't let me dishonor You or be disobedient by not sharing enough.

Keep me from wanting to look good in front of others. Give me the freedom of writing without any filter but Your Spirit. Use me and all my mistakes and failings to reach others for Your glory. Amen.

A Balanced Life For Writers

Trust in the LORD forever, For in GOD the LORD, we have an everlasting Rock (Isaiah 26:4 NASB).

Everywhere we turn we're being urged to find balance. In advertising we're given soothing images of candles, yoga, exercise, places to get away, etc. etc. etc. In my life, I try to balance writing, marketing, family, friends, church ... all good activities, but too much is still too much. No amount of scented candles or stretching can help a writer who is struggling to find time to write.

As I try once again to wrest control from the chaos that is my schedule I've come to a startling revelation.

A balanced life doesn't look like we think it should.

I'm learning that balance isn't an exterior stability, it's an interior poise. I don't care how strict we are about planning, diet, exercise, even environment, times of chaos will erupt. We know this is true by experience, but more importantly we know it by looking at the life Jesus lived.

As we march through the New Testament, we see Jesus when the crowds are pushing in, clamoring for attention. We see His followers disappoint Him. We even see times when He is faced with unexpected—in a human sense—death.

Within this outward chaos, we also see a perfect example of living a life of balance. And it has nothing to do with what's going on around Him, much less planning, diet, exercise, or environment. It has everything to do with His absolute passion for allowing God to direct His steps.

So how do we imitate Jesus? We draw closer to God. It's that simple and that difficult. In the past, as deadlines crowded in, my inclination was to spend more time writing and less time with God. It's embarrassing to share that about me, but it's true. Now, the busier I am, the more deliberate I am about my time in the Word and in prayer. I've learned—the hard way—the only way to come through the chaos is at the side of Jesus.

So as I launch full-force into busyness and deadlines, I'm remembering the lessons I've learn. I'm looking to God for balance, not at what's happening around me. Care to join me?

Forging a Creative Connection

Balance is an inward poise, not an outward stability. And the guide to true balance is found only in God. So how do we grab hold of His steadying hand when our world is rocked out of control? By spending time in His presence.

Here are the supplies you'll need:

- ☑ This book
- ☑ Pen or pencil
- ☑ Optional
- ☑ Colored Pencils, Markers and/or crayons
- ☑ Stickers
- ☑ Washi Tape

On the next page, write the BALANCE across the top. Then draw a line dividing the rest of the page vertically—you'll now have a right half and a left half.

On the left half, list three to five people, events, duties, attitudes, or chores that are currently pulling you off balance in your writing. Now pray. Ask God to lead to you to three to five Bible verses that answer those disturbances. You can use a concordance to look up words, do a search on the Internet, or call a friend.

A Prayer for Time to Write

The LORD directs the steps of the godly. He delights in every detail of their lives (Psalm 37:23 NLT).

Dear Lord, You are the one who orders my days and directs my steps. But at the moment, it feels like no one is in control of this chaos. You've called me to write, but I have absolutely no time to be obedient.

I desperately need Your help. I want to follow You, but I can't find a way to squeeze another second out of my overloaded schedule. I need Your wisdom and a fairly good-sized miracle to make this work.

When I accepted that You made me a writer, I had such dreams of what that would look like. I envisioned hours on end where I communed with You and the words flowed like water. I saw my life gently rearranged as You made room in it for me to write.

What I've got is a bulging schedule that forces me to sneak in five minutes here and fifteen minutes there to write. I really don't think this is what I signed up for.

I'm discovering that part of the problem is me. I'm not making room to follow where You lead. Help me make wiser choices and pare down my schedule so I have time to write. But even when I do make wise choices, unexpected catastrophe strikes. Illness, power-outages, and other unexpected happenings work to keep me from my appointed task.

At times it seems everything in the universe is bent to keeping me from writing.

That's the way of it, isn't it? When Your followers agree to Your will, the enemy steps in to bring chaos. Lord You are bigger than my schedule and more powerful than the prince of this world. If Your purpose means I must write in the moments, I commit to that. But I'm also believing You will order my days and give me the wisdom to choose what things fill my life. Amen.

The Freedom of Transparency

*For it is not you who speak, but it is the Spirit of your
Father who speaks in you (Matthew 10:20 NASB).*

The past few years I've done a good bit of public speaking. Since I'm a writer, you might assume
that's a good thing. It probably should be, except for
one thing—it's *way* out of my comfort zone. As a
matter of fact, if I wasn't certain God was asking me
to share, I wouldn't be doing it.

Even the knowledge that I'm being obedient
doesn't help a lot. I'm just not comfortable with the
spotlight shining on me. It feels wrong—like I'm calling attention to myself rather than to God.

The only way I've found to mitigate this feeling is
by drawing a clear contrast between the mess God
has to work through—that would be me—and the
results of His miraculous effort. But for this strategy

to be effective I have to be willing to show myself honestly—with all my flaws.

At first being transparent was as scary as the whole get-up-on-stage bit.

But after a time or two of letting people see through the me I wished I was—and tried to pretend to be—and directly at who I am, I discovered something.

There is an amazing freedom in being yourself.

I no longer have to keep up the pretense of being spiritual, or an expert, or anything else. Instead, I can relax and *be*—resting in whatever God wants to bring out.

This transparency also takes the pressure off those who are watching me. They aren't misled into believing they must be something they aren't. They don't have to start out already *good enough* to qualify to get better. They can start right where they were.

And in the midst of all this, I realize I have the ability to achieve one of my deepest desires—to be invisible.

Because through this God has taught me that transparent is just another word for invisible.

When I'm truly transparent, God can shine through in all His glory. There are no smudges of me to get in the way.

What smudges are you holding onto? Take a chance and join me in the freedom of transparency.

Forging a
Creative Connection

Today we're going to explore what God has to say about who He created you to be. There is so much freedom found in taking off the masks and leaning in to the person you were meant to be.

Here are the supplies you'll need:

- ☑ This book
- ☑ Bible
- ☑ Pen or pencil
- ☑ Optional
- ☑ Colored Pencils, Markers and/or crayons
- ☑ Stickers
- ☑ Washi Tape

This exercise is as simple as it is difficult. First read Psalm 139 and consider how carefully God created you to be exactly who you are. Use the next page to journal your answer to this question:

How would you manage your writing life differently if you knew publication was guaranteed and no one would judge you negatively for what you had to say or how you said it?

A Prayer for True Freedom

In the same way the Spirit also helps our weakness;
for we do not know how to pray as we should, but the
Spirit Himself intercedes for us with groanings too deep
for words (Romans 8:26 NASB).

Dear Lord, I'm discovering that I'm bound up, struggling with the fact that I'm an inept writer. There are hundreds of others who are more talented and have more powerful stories to tell.

You chose me to write for You, but it seems so illogical. My insight isn't as profound as others, and I'm slow to learn the lessons.

As I speak these words out loud, I find myself noticing a theme. I'm worried about *me*. And the focus of this endeavor isn't me, it's You.

It doesn't matter how mediocre I am. My goal is to become totally invisible so that when someone looks at me or something I write, they see only You. I've been going about this all wrong, trying to be the person You need me to be to accomplish Your purpose.

Your purpose is to use me where I am right now, and then tomorrow, where I am then. I don't have to strive to become something more. You are all I need. Amen.

Don't Get Caught in the Comparison Trap

*He says, Don't be afraid, because I have saved you. I
have called you by name, and you are mine
(Isaiah 43:1 NCV).*

I had just finished a wonderful weekend at writers
conference and was driving home. I was evaluating
what I'd experienced and I noticed something important—something that has stuck with me. Across
the board, we writers are way too hard on ourselves.
We're constantly comparing ourselves to each other.
No matter where we are in our career, we're always
looking at the person ahead of us.

We need to quit looking ahead and start looking up.

It's easy to get caught up in the comparison
mentality. There's so much about our industry that

depends on the opinions of others. We check to see how many views our articles get, how many followers our blogs have, and/or how many stars the reviewer gave our latest book.

These things can undermine and sometimes even totally destroy our perspective, not to mention our confidence. Because, let's face it, there is always someone willing to point out what we did wrong or could have done better.

If we're not careful, we can get to the point where we value what others are saying *about* us more than what God is doing *through* us.

So how do we stay focused in this crazy writing world where everyone seems altogether too eager to pass judgment? I think the key to thriving in this hyper-competitive environment is to keep focused on what and especially on Who matters.

He knows my name. God recognizes my face. He knows my character.

When I focus God's Word and His opinion, my heart stays safe and protected. That's when I'm insulated from a worldly perspective determined to destroy anything God has called good.

Forging a
Creative Connection

There is so much to be learned by creating a writing vision board. This exercise will lead you through the process of making a small one in this book and later you may choose to make a larger one or even use the instructions to create a notebook of writing vision boards that highlight all the different aspects of writing that you love.

Here are the supplies you'll need:

☑ This book
☑ Paper with words and pictures on it. This can be magazines, newspapers, scrapbook paper, even print outs.
☑ Scissors
☑ Stickers

☑ Washi Tape

☑ Glue

☑ Optional

☑ Colored Pencils, Markers and/or crayons

Begin this exercise with prayer, asking God to lead you to revelation about who He created you to be as a writer. Don't be afraid to include your hopes and dreams as well as the things you already incorporate into who you are as a writer. When putting together this project, remember that there is no *wrong* way to do it. Don't stress if you find yourself assembling it out of order. Here are the steps to include when building a vision board:

1. Step One: Choose something on which to assemble your vision board. It can be a piece of cardboard, poster board, scrapbook paper—even a page in a notebook. Just remember that you'll be adhering things to the board so it needs to be sturdy enough to support the weight.

2. Step Two: Begin your vision board by choosing a Bible verse or phrase that speaks to you. My latest vision board began

with my tagline – Find Your Voice, Live Your Story.

3. Step Three: Browse through the resources you've assembled (magazines, newspapers, etc) and begin cutting and tearing out phrases and pictures that speak to you. You're looking for a variety—images, text, and size. You may be struck by a word, or a color, or the expression on someone's face. If you feel like it fits, add it to your collection.

4. Step Four: Start laying out your collection on your board. I begin with the bigger pieces first. When I have an idea of where I want to put some things, I begin gluing and taping. Some items I will glue onto the paper. Other treasures I may adhere with decorative washi tape or stickers.

5. Step Five: After I have adhered these images to the board, I go back and evaluate my thoughts as I look at the board. I use this time to also begin to personalize it. I may write a word or a thought next to a picture, or draw something, or even add some color to an area that feels too empty.

6. Step Six: I find a place to display my board. I usually pin it up on my bulletin board in my office. Over the course of a few days I will finalize it—possibly adding a few new concepts and beliefs. I love to hang on to my vision boards and see how God has grown me as a writer and in my calling.

A Prayer for Contentment

But godliness with contentment is great gain
(1 Timothy 6:6 NIV).

Dear Lord, I'm worried about the reach of my writing. I know that I need to share my words with others, but no matter how hard I try, I can't seem to achieve the numbers I think I need. There are days and even weeks when I feel like I'm writing into a black hole and no one's even noticing. Am I wasting my time?

Give me the encouragement I need to stay motivated. Show me that what I'm doing is accomplishing the purpose You planned.

Help me find balance in this crazy calling. Instead of striving, I want to be content where I am. I don't want to give up, but I want to focus on You and what You want to say through me rather than growing numbers.

Don't ever let me forget that each of those numbers is a person—someone You love. Let me see the value in smaller groups. Help me avoid the comparison trap. Let me lean into You and fully embrace the journey You have planned for me and my writing. Amen.

The Day the Truth Set My Writing Free

Then you will know the truth, and the truth will set you free (John 8:32 NIV).

*N*ow I have to confess, usually I can only take so much *truth* when it comes to my writing. And as exciting as writing conferences are, there tends to be—in my humble opinion—a surfeit of truth going on there.

Everyone you meet has an opinion, especially when it comes to your writing and how it should be fixed. Add to that the late nights, adrenalin rush of meetings, and a schedule jam packed with classes and you have a recipe for emotional disaster.

I found myself on that rollercoaster at a large conference back in 2009. Luckily it wasn't my first big conference, but it was by far the largest I'd ever attended.

But two days in, on a Saturday morning, after an unusually good night's rest, worship was a wonderful time of hearing from God.

The worship team led us in several praise songs, but the one that resonated with me focused on the freedom we have in Christ. I found myself asking God how I could hang on to that freedom in a day I knew would be packed with unexpected highs and lows.

Frequently, in the past, I've found the conference and the week following, a time of bondage. I've felt trapped by expectations of others and the obvious shortcomings within myself.

As I prayed, asking if somehow this time could be different I felt my spirit vibrate with God's answer. His answer was to remind me that He gave me this story—for this time. He didn't choose anyone else, He chose me. And I felt that today He would confirm His trust in me.

After the worship time, I went straight to my fifteen-minute appointment with an editor. As I sat down, I felt slightly nervous, but nothing like I usually felt. The editor listened as I gave him a brief pitch, and then asked to see the first few pages of the manuscript. He read for a moment and asked if I'd like editorial feedback.

I felt myself swallow hard—here it came—more of that truth. But I replaced my fear with a picture of the word freedom and nodded. As he began marking up my pages and explaining sections that needed to be cut, I felt an unearthly peace. Here it was—God's confirmation.

The editor stopped talking and looked at me strangely. "You're taking this awfully well."

That was when I realized I had a huge grin on my face. I'm sure it must have briefly crossed his mind that I was some sort of a nutcase or maybe he was the butt of a joke and this wasn't really my manuscript.

The truth was that his revisions filled me with joy. The parts he removed were those that I'd let others—against my better judgment—talk me into adding. When he was done, I was left with the story exactly the way God had given it to me.

That day I found the freedom that God's truth brings—and even more importantly—the confidence to believe in God's work in me and in my ability to carry it out.

Are you concerned about what's He's given you? Today I challenge you to ask for God's confirmation. His answer may surprise and delight you—it certainly did me.

Forging a Creative Connection

Many years ago I created a personal writing bucket list. It consisted of endeavors I wanted to accomplish, places I wanted to visit, and people I wanted to meet. There is power in writing out dreams and goals, praying over them, and committing them to the Lord. Today you're going to do it.

Here are the supplies you'll need:

☑ This book
☑ Pen or pencil
☑ Optional
☑ Colored Pencils, Markers and/or crayons
☑ Stickers
☑ Washi Tape

Use the following page to write out your bucket list. As you make the list, pray over it, asking God to help you fulfill it. Decorate the page any way you choose. Then keep this book handy. As you fulfill the list, write the date beside it. Come back and check in every six months to a year and mark how God is working in your life.

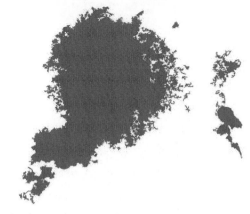

A Prayer About Truth

Whoever heeds life-giving correction will be at home among the wise (Proverbs 15:31 NIV).

Dear Lord, I want to know the truth about my ability as a writer, but I'm so fearful when I ask someone to look at what I've written. It hurts when someone criticizes what I've done. It makes me worry that I'll never be good enough. Criticism makes me uncertain. I've invested so much for so long that I don't want to give it up. I love what I do. But I cannot continue without Your confirmation.

I want to improve, but how do I know what I'm hearing from others is the truth? I'm torn between feeling like You are enough and knowing that You expect me continue to grow in this area. I need to learn how to stay to true to what You've asked me to write and still make it better. Give me Your perspective and Your truth.

Help me discern the truth between what's spoken about my writing. Keep me from jumping immediately to defensiveness. Even when I disagree, show me if there is any part of the criticism that comes from You to make my writing better.

Give me grace toward the ones who offer well-meaning criticism. Don't let me take offense or speak harshly. Guide me into walking in Your truth as I learn what it means to write with excellence. Amen.

3 Scripture Prescriptions to Meet God Where You Are

There are very few of us who wouldn't go see a doctor when we're ill. But for some reason, when our souls are ailing, we often avoid seeking out the recommendations of our heavenly physician. This list of Bible verses are what I like to term, *scripture prescriptions*.

I recommend you don't simply scan them, but use the following pages to decorate and write out what God is saying to you through each of them.

I also urge you to copy them onto index cards and tape them around your home and car. The constant reminder that God has an answer to what is wrong can bring us the peace we're so desperately craving.

Therefore put on the full armor of God, so that when the day of evil comes, you may be able to stand your ground, and after you have done everything, to stand (Ephesians 6:13 NIV).

But the Helper will teach you everything and will cause you to remember all that I told you. This Helper is the Holy Spirit whom the Father will send in my name (John 14:26 NCV).

The Lord will fight for you; you need only to be still (Exodus 14:14 NIV).

Chapter Five

Fortifying Faith

Faith must be the foundation for anyone following the writing road. This journey takes us from mountaintop experiences with God all around us, into the darkest valley where we feel we'll never find God again. Only a solid core of faith keeps us moving through these ups and downs.

Writers are creatives, and for the most part, that means we're also tied to our emotions. We experience life with our hearts and that's what makes us able to do what we do. However, it also makes us vulnerable. Our feelings can be deceptive when it comes to evaluating our journey and our progress. Faith in the truth of God will keep us grounded and anchored to the only One whose opinion matters.

So go forth and experience all God has for you. Embrace the joy and even the sorrow and use your

words to interpret and apply context to this world.
Then always come home to rest in the completeness
and joy of God.

Write in Faith

Now faith is confidence in what we hope for and assurance about what we do not see (Hebrews 11:1 NIV).

This verse is one of the first verses I learned when I began memorizing scripture. But until today, I had never thought about applying it to my writing. This morning I was texting back and forth with a fellow writer, trying to encourage her to move forward and leave the result up to God.

You see, November is National Novel Writing Month. Or in the vocabulary of writers, NaNoWriMo. The goal is to write fifty-thousand words in one month. The plan was started to help writers get a story down, *before* editing. A good idea, but the schedule carries with it a lot of pressure. That burden was what my friend was dealing with.

So I texted that my friend should sit down at the computer and *write in faith.* As I hit send, the words were highlighted and hit me like a message from God. I knew, in that moment, that I desperately needed to take my own advice.

Let me explain. To get ready for NaNoWriMo, I've been working hard at mapping out a fiction manuscript. I've gotten to know my characters, researched the location, even brainstormed the major plot points.

But still I was overcome with doubt and indecision every time I sat down to write.

I had forgotten that, prepared or not, the outcome of my writing is in God's capable hands. Sure I need to be obedient and do my homework. But then, I needed to leave the results up to him.

Even the *small* results.

He's in charge of how each scene turns out, as well as how the book turns out, and even whether it's published or not. And his supervision doesn't only apply to fiction—He has plans for our devotions, articles, blog posts, even our social media updates. Beyond that, He cares about the people who will read and *when* they read it.

My part is small—obedience. I know, it's *not* easy, but the big stuff is Gods. It's not my place to think too far ahead in the process.

So that day I sat down and wrote with this revelation in mind—and the joy returned.

The pressure had disappeared and the fun of playing with the words returned. So join me, as I move forward—Write in faith!

Forging a
Creative Connection

I absolutely love playing with words. One of my favorite method is by writing haiku poetry.

Here are the supplies you'll need:

- ☑ This book
- ☑ Pen or pencil
- ☑ Optional
- ☑ Colored Pencils, Markers and/or crayons
- ☑ Stickers
- ☑ Washi Tape

Use the next page to write your poem. Follow the standard Haiku format (shown below) and write a poem exploring what writing in faith means to you.

For some extra fun, pair your poem with an image and share it on social media and tag #soulcare.

First line, 5 syllables

Second line, 7 syllables

Third line, 5 syllables

After you finish, decorate your page any way you wish.

A Prayer for Deeper Faith

*So faith comes from hearing, and hearing by the word
of Christ (Romans 10:17 NASB).*

Dear Lord, I'm struggling with my writing.
I'm discouraged and need a fresh infusion of Your
strength. Increase my faith and don't let me keep spi-
raling down this road of negativity.

I love writing—at least I used to—but now it
seems that there is so much tied to it that I can't
feel that love. In my mind, everything I do is tied to
results and I know that can't be right. The results are
up to You. My part is obedience. Help me turn off
my mind.

Help me redirect my anxious thoughts into
peaceful paths. Give me a clear line between my
part and Your part. I want to return to the freedom
and joy of concentrating on the words and what You

want to say through me. Take away my stress about where the words will go and who will read them.

Let me see how my words are being used by You—not enough for me to become prideful—but enough to lead me into a deeper faith. Return my joy of writing for You. It's amazing that You would want to use me as part of Your work in this world. Remove the worry and doubt and replace it with faith. Amen.

Faith, For the Word People

For we walk by faith, not by sight
(2 Corinthians 5:7 HCSB).

As writers, we have chosen to follow a difficult path. I remember, after a particularly hard week, my husband remarked that he wished I'd chosen another career, something simple—like becoming a movie star.

His comparison was more appropriate than he realized. Success, for both career choices appears, from the outside at least, to rely on being popular with a lot of people. Reaching the top seems to come and go with the whims of an unknown audience. We struggle and strive for numbers—likes on our Facebook pages, followers on Twitter, and ultimately sales numbers. We seek to please our readers, our publishers, even other writers.

We are word people—caged and captured by numbers.

But when we have chosen this path at God's calling, our focus needs to be somewhere other than those who will read our words. Our audience is an audience of One, and it is to Him and Him alone that we owe our allegiance. He will dictate, with wisdom far beyond our own, who will read our words and the reach they will have. And I for one, am well pleased to leave my destiny in His capable hands.

So today I encourage you to seek out the joy of your audience, because I know He is well pleased by your obedience to follow His call. Let Him lavish you with praise and protect you from worry. Leave the numbers to Him and concentrate only on the words.

Forging a Creative Connection

This exercise will introduce us to the ABCs of God.

Here are the supplies you'll need:

- ☑ This book
- ☑ Pen or pencil
- ☑ Optional
- ☑ Colored Pencils, Markers and/or crayons
- ☑ Stickers
- ☑ Washi Tape

The foundation of our faith comes from knowing God, which is also the foundation of our writing. Today you're going to ask God to reveal Himself to you through the alphabet. In your journal, write a word describing God for each letter of the alphabet, write a word. For example, A might be Almighty, B might be Beautiful, etc. Use the following page and make your list. You may have to get creative on some of the more unusual letters like X and Z, but I know God has an amazing revelation in store for you.

A Prayer For Renewal

But those who trust the Lord will find new strength. They will be strong like eagles soaring upward on wings; they will walk and run without getting tired (Isaiah 40:31 CEV).

Dearest Lord, You created me this way. You gave me the yearning to put words on paper. But now I've lost my joy.

Remind me of how You've opened the floodgates of words. Let them once again pour forth as I strive to be an obedient child and allow Your message to find its voice in me.

You are the living water that runs through my soul. Yet I feel like my access to You is blocked. Help me see clearly what is keeping me from creating. Once again inspire me with Your thoughts and Your dreams. Don't let that creative part of me shrivel up and die.

Put others in my life to speak Your words of encouragement. Use them, not as a source of competition, but as comforters and fellow travelers. Don't let me give weight to discouraging thoughts and voices that populate my mind. Replace my doubts with a new confidence that will withstand any trial.

Hold me close and whisper thoughts and ideas into my heart. Don't ever let Your voice be drowned out by my struggle. Instead, give me again the wings to soar as Your mouthpiece. Hold me close and guide my fingers to form the words that You will use to touch a world that's in pain. Amen.

Are You Skydiving or Flying?

Now to Him who is able to do far more abundantly beyond all that we ask or think, according to the power that works within us (Ephesians 3:20 ESV).

Sometimes (more often than not) I get caught up in the process of life. I'm an analytical sort of person, and I'm definitely a planner. With every project I tackle, I make plans, trying to anticipate any possible potholes and pitfalls. I build timelines and set expectations.

I'm also a recovering perfectionist.

For years I didn't realize I was a perfectionist, but I definitely am. My perfectionism shows itself in strange ways. In the past, it has kept me from trying anything I thought I couldn't succeed at. For me, failure wasn't an option. That translated into a hurdle that kept me from pursuing my dreams.

Truthfully, perfection is an issue that continues to crop up from time to time. (I can anticipate the snickers this engenders in my family and close friends as they read this.)

In the past, I've gone to great lengths to build in safeguards that keep failure at bay when I tackle a difficult project. I always thought of my safeguards as packing a parachute—a built-in safety net that would keep me from crashing and burning.

Then one day I felt a metaphoric tap on the shoulder from the Holy Spirit. He asked me a question I've never forgotten.

Are you skydiving or flying?

You see God is in the business of helping us to fly. He's not interested in skydiving, and He has no need of parachutes. Sure we need to prepare to fly, but packing a parachute isn't one of the items to pack. God wants us to fly free, chasing the dreams He's set into our hearts. His plan doesn't include the encumbrances of safety nets and parachutes. When He's in control, safeguards just baggage that can hold us tethered to the ground.

So whatever dream you're chasing, leave the parachute at home and get ready to fly.

Forging a
Creative Connection

*F*lying—even in the context of writing—can be a scary prospect. It involves saying yes to writing what we've never done and going places we've never gone before. I think it's time to explore the possibilities behind the word yes.

Here are the supplies you'll need:

- ☑ This book
- ☑ Pen or pencil
- ☑ Optional
- ☑ Colored Pencils, Markers and/or crayons
- ☑ Stickers
- ☑ Washi Tape

On the next page, write the word, YES, across the top. Now consider something you've always thought about doing with your writing and were afraid to try. Write all the positive consequences that *could* happen if you said yes. Now spend some time in prayer, asking God to give you the courage and the opportunity to say yes.

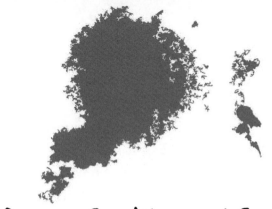

A Prayer For Wings of Faith

You know that you learn to endure by having your faith tested (James 1:3 CEV).

Dear Lord, as I travel this writing road, I confess I've been preparing to skydive, instead of fly. Without realizing it, I've packed only items I'll need for quick jumps of faith. I've ignored what I need to have if I'm to let go and fly.

I confess that flying scares me. On the surface, soaring with You sounds amazing, but as I look deeper into what that entails, I'm less certain. I thrive with lists and plans and concrete goals that are measurable and trackable. Flying with You would mean following air currents I couldn't see or touch. I'd have to let go of expectations and rely wholly on You. I want to have the faith to fly with You, but even flying is something You're going to have to do. I tiptoe to the edge of the cliff, but I'm too afraid to hold Your hand and jump.

Even though I'm not quite there, I'm asking You to take me to that place. Equip me to make that leap. Give me the desire to trust only in You. I know You want me to have goals and dreams, but You don't want them to be my focus. Right now those goals and dreams are tethers, keeping me tied to the ground.

Give me wings of faith. Show me how to cut those ties and take my writing to the next level of faith and purpose. Amen.

Have You Joined the Choir?

Then we'll be a choir—not our voices only, but our very lives singing in harmony in a stunning anthem to the God and Father of our Master Jesus! (Romans 15:6 THE MESSAGE).

I get the opportunity to talk to a lot of writers. And we all have one big thing in common—insecurity.

It's actually a trait I see in a lot of people, not only writers. I used to struggle, wondering how someone with as little to offer as me could make a difference in this world. I mean, as a writer who's a Christian, how could I be as impactful as others who are already having an impact.

There are lots of logical arguments for and against this lack of confidence. But, for me, none of them ever helped. None of them explained why God would use me when He has so many more qualified.

Really does the world need one more Christian writer or blogger, or am I just adding to the noise.

I finally got smart and one morning, during my quiet time, took the question to God. I wanted Him to either confirm His calling on my life or not. Here's what God had to say, not in literal words, but in a new way of thinking about my concern of adding to the noise in the world.

He used the analogy of a choir.

He showed me that He has thousands of voices out there who are His choir. And as in musical choir, the music is more beautiful with more than one soprano or more than one alto. The same holds true with the chorus He's put together to spread His message. He uses thousands of us, many with the same message, but a unique voice to make up the sections of His choir. He assured me that while I may not be a soloist, He still misses me when I'm not there.

I'm one voice, but when He directs, the music is divine!

Forging a
Creative Connection

*L*earning to listen is a skill that all writers need to master. Even though it doesn't involve music directly, well-crafted sentences have a rhythm and flow. Experienced writers know how to vary this rhythm to enhance the mood of the piece. Today we're going to practice this skill.

Here are the supplies you'll need:

- ☑ This book
- ☑ A Notebook or journal
- ☑ Pen or pencil
- ☑ Access to music: radio, stereo, online streaming, etc

Optional
- ☑ Colored Pencils, Markers and/or crayons

☑ Stickers
☑ Washi Tape

Find a station or a selection of music that is instrumental (no words) and have it playing in the background. At the top of the next page, write out the following verse:

My heart overflows with a pleasing theme; I address my verses to the king; my tongue is like the pen of a ready scribe (Psalm 45:1 ESV).

Now spend some time freewriting about what it means to be a *ready scribe*. Let the rhythm of the music inspire your words and your word choices.

Prayer About Letting My Faith Sing

Sing to him, sing praise to him; tell of all his wonderful acts (Psalm 105:2 NIV).

Dear Lord, why would you choose to use someone like me? There are others who are more eloquent in their writing, more wise in their application, and have more experience. My audience is precious, but tiny. I don't feel like there's anything unique about what I have to say.

I am thrilled to feel Your call on my life—to think that You may have designed me for such a time as this. But it feels like all I have to say has been said before. I worry that I may have missed the message You intended me to share. Why do You need one more person saying the same thing?

Give me confirmation that I'm on the right path. Show me how my message can impact Your kingdom. I'm not asking for a huge audience, I'm happy where I am, as long as I'm in the middle of Your will. Don't let me grow discouraged. Instead keep me steadfast and firm in all You've called me to do.

You are the reason behind my words and the hope in my heart. When I feel Your Spirit whisper words into my soul, I'm most happy. Sharing Your gift to even a small group brings me joy. Help my faith grow stronger and sing the song You intended. Amen.

Remember God Takes the Scenic Route

Trust in the Lord with all your heart, and do not rely on your own understanding; think about Him in all your ways, and He will guide you on the right paths (Proverbs 3:5-6 HCSB).

I grew up during the 60s and 70s, in a family that loved to travel. Some of my earliest memories are of traveling across the United States, looking at life from the rear view window of a Volkswagen Beetle. When my sister was born, our family went from three to four and our parents traded in the Volkswagen Beetle for a Volkswagen Bus.

Oh the places we visited.

I've been out west in a blizzard so fierce we had to scrape ice from the inside of the windows. I've cooked an egg on the pavement in Death Valley, and spent several nights camping on top of what used to be Mount St. Helens. But only a small percentage of our time on the road was spent on major highways.

No, Daddy's preferred method of travel was the *Scenic Route*. It became a family joke. We all knew better than to wonder out loud where a side road went. That was all the excuse our father needed to head out toward unknown adventure. Sometimes that adventure was exciting, ending with amazing vistas and views that my photographer father captured on film.

Other times . . . well . . . not so much.

I remember one afternoon all too well. We'd headed down a road and got stuck in the mud. The road was little more than a dirt path. It was decades before cell phones. All we could do was pray someone else had a taste for adventure. Sure enough, just as the sun was racing toward the horizon, a huge truck, complete with towing package, rounded the bend. He was as surprised to see us as we were to see him.

He pulled us out in no time, refusing the money my dad tried to give him. When mom pushed, asking to know why he'd come down this road, he tipped back his cowboy hat and scratched his head. "I can't really say. It just seemed like something I needed to do."

That was one of my first introductions to the power of prayer, and I've never forgotten it. I've also never forgotten something else. The joy is in the journey, not only the destination.

Through the years, I've come to realize God is a lot like my daddy. (I know it's really the other way around, but humor me. I'm making a point here.) My heavenly Father also likes to take the scenic route. He'll drag me places I think are miles out of the way, putting my goal further and further from reach. Then boom, we round a corner and there stands what I was aiming for all along.

Or He leads me down a path that leaves me bogged down for months, and it's only when look back that I see that time of stillness was what I needed. So often it's in the mud that my hardest lessons and greatest joys have been realized.

Forging a Creative Connection

As I've said over and over in this book, each of us is a unique creation. God has a plan and a purpose for our lives—and our writing. While it's important to grow and explore, we flourish best from a foundation of being who God planned us to be. Today we're going to begin writing an author mission statement.

Here are the supplies you'll need:

- ☑ This book
- ☑ Pen or pencil
- ☑ Journal or notebook
- ☑ Access to music: radio, stereo, online streaming, etc
- ☑ Optional

☑ Colored Pencils, Markers and/or crayons

☑ Stickers

☑ Washi Tape

Crafting an author mission statement isn't usually a quick project. But it's vital that each writer has one. It will help us evaluate opportunities and give us confidence to move forward because we know who we are.

In your journal or notebook, begin the process by answering each question below in a single sentence.

- What do you do? Yes, you write. But go deeper than that.
- Who do you do it for?
- What makes you unique?
- What can your readers expect?

Play with the statements you've written. Some of them may meld together into a single sentence. After you've got an idea of where you're headed, add an "I believe" statement to the beginning.

Here is my author mission statement:

I believe God has a purpose for everyone's unique story. I encourage others to live that story by telling stories of my own— through words and pictures. I'm a writer who feels lost without her camera and a reluctant speaker who loves to encourage an audience. All my books point to the transformational possibilities inside each of us when we tap into our God-given strengths.

This statement helps me evaluate opportunities, stay on track with my purpose, and lean into God as I become more of who He designed me to be.

A Prayer for the Dry Times

Call to Me and I will answer you, and I will tell you great and mighty things, which you do not know (Jeremiah 33:3 NASB).

Dear Lord, I'm struggling with frustration. I've submitted my writing many places—contests, periodicals, agents, and publishers—and I'm not seeing the results I expected. I'm not even getting any helpful feedback. Have I somehow missed Your will for my writing?

I'm not expecting instant success, but it seems like I'm getting nowhere. I've been stuck in this wilderness for so long. Help me find Your purpose in this. Surely You didn't bring me to this place just to turn my dreams to dust.

As I search for You in this dry time I admit I *am* learning lessons. I see that I've been guilty of judging the worth of my writing by what others say. Instead I need to come to You for my confirmation. I'm trying to disconnect my expectations from my obedience, but it's so hard.

You've done so much in my life that I want others to see. I don't want this for my glory, but for Yours. Help me learn how to balance my zeal for You with patience for Your timing. Give me something to hang onto that proves I'm on the path You have planned.

I know I can trust You with my dreams. Right now I'm recommitting myself to Your timing and Your results. You will never abandon me and I will continue to follow You, no matter where that path leads or how long it takes. Amen.

3 Scripture Prescriptions to Meet God Where You Are

There are very few of us who wouldn't go see a doctor when we're ill. But for some reason, when our souls are ailing, we often avoid seeking out the recommendations of our heavenly physician. This list of Bible verses are what I like to term, *scripture prescriptions*.

I recommend you don't simply scan them, but use the following pages to decorate and write out what God is saying to you through each of them.

I also urge you to copy them onto index cards and tape them around your home and car. The constant reminder that God has an answer to what is wrong can bring us the peace we're so desperately craving.

Nothing is impossible for God! (Luke 1:37 CEV).

Look among the nations! Observe! Be astonished! Wonder! Because I am doing something in your days— You would not believe if you were told)Habakkuk 1:5 NASB).

This is why You are great, Lord GOD. There is no one like You, and there is no God besides You, as all we have heard confirms (2 Samuel 7:22 HCSB).

About the Author

Edie Melson is a woman of faith with ink-stained fingers who is known to quip that's she's creative out of self-defense. No surprise since she's the daughter of an artist-mother and musician-turned-photographer-father, and admits she'd have been a disgrace if she hadn't been true her own creativity."

As an author, blogger, and speaker she's encouraged and challenged audiences across the country and around the world. Her numerous books reflect her passion to help others develop the strength of their God-given gifts and apply them to their lives.

She's a leading professional within the publishing industry and travels to numerous conferences as a popular keynote, writing instructor, and mentor. Her blog for writers, <u>The Write Conversation</u>, reaches thousands each month and is a Writer's Digest Best 101 Websites for Writers. She's a board member of the <u>Advanced Writers and Speakers Association</u>, the Social Media Director for <u>Southern Writers</u>

Magazine, as well as the director of the <u>Blue Ridge</u> <u>Mountains Christian Writers Conference.</u>

She and husband Kirk have been married 38+ years and raised three sons. They live in the foothills of the Blue Ridge Mountains in SC where they love to hike and wander the mountains. Connect with her on her website, www.EdieMelson.com and through social media.

Bible Translations Used